Rachel

W9-CAD-741

Bibliographies

D. W. KRUMMEL

Bibliographies

Their Aims and Methods

MANSELL PUBLISHING LIMITED
London   New York

First Published 1984 by
Mansell Publishing Limited
(A subsidiary of The H. W. Wilson Company)
6 All Saints Street, London N1 9RL, England
950 University Avenue, Bronx, New York 10452, U.S.A.

British Library Cataloguing in Publication Data

Krummel, D. W.
  Bibliographies,
  1. Bibliography
  I. Title
  010   Z1001

    ISBN 0-7201-1687-2

Library of Congress Cataloging in Publication Data

Krummel, Donald William, 1929-
  Bibliographies, their aims and methods.

  Bibliography: p.
  Includes index.
  1. Bibliography. 2. Bibliography—Methodology.
  3. Bibliography—Bibliography. I. Title.
  Z1001.K86 1984   011'.44   83-22177
  ISBN 0-7201-1687-2

Filmset by Latimer Trend & Company Ltd, Plymouth
Printed and bound in Great Britain

Contents

List of Reference Sources

Preface

When a compiler expects to commit dozens, perhaps hundreds or even thousands of hours assembling a bibliography, another few hours ought to be spent planning the project and 'modeling' the product in the light of the experiences of earlier compilers. And as bibliographical control over the world's recorded knowledge is envisioned, the role of bibliographies, past, present, and future, ought to be taken into account. These are the two premises that underlie this text.

This may all sound very reasonable; but recent experience has led me to question the political wisdom of preparing a book that addresses these matters. The text will no doubt be belaboured from two sides. Many of my humanistic brethren will see only the busy-work. Bibliography has little to do with the proper study of mankind; it never did entail any significant creative efforts, and with computers here now never will. On the other hand, many of my associates in the library and hi-tech information communities will question the cost of service to highly specialized audiences through bibliographies, perhaps even the objective as well. The lateral cross-fire notwithstanding, I should like to think bibliographies will continue to play an essential role in providing access to recorded knowledge; in all events the compiler's perspectives as expressed here may clarify some of the basic matters that will always need to be addressed by those who work with bibliographical records of all kinds.

Compilers, meanwhile, will often call on technical specialities — mostly in fields of library and information science, or in matters of processing, presentation, and publication—that are highly developed in their own right. In deference to the common needs of compilers in general, I have very briefly summarized some topics that, for particular compilers, might appropriately benefit from whole chapters. Readers should be alerted, if not by noticeably qualified prose, more clearly by the interpolated sections of selected bibliographical references (*see* p. vii above).

I am particularly grateful to W. Boyd Rayward, G. Thomas Tanselle and Frank O. Williams, who read the major early draft of this text and offered invaluable criticisms; and to John E. Duncan and Elbie Spivack for their sympathetic editorial support in London. I also owe thanks to the students in my introductory bibliography courses, whose assignments have provided so much valuable grist for the mill (if not in fact fodder for the cannon); and to Drs Kenneth Lavender, William McCully, Jr, David Zubatsky and Richard Y. Meier, who provided much useful assistance through the support of the Graduate School of Library and Information Science and the Research Board of the University of Illinois.

CHAPTER I

Introduction

ENUMERATIVE BIBLIOGRAPHIES

The purpose of this book is to describe the ideal practices and features that characterize our most respected bibliographies; to suggest by contrast what makes other lists, their usefulness notwithstanding, essentially flawed; and to propose the special functions of bibliographies in guiding readers to the texts they need to know.

Bibliographies are one component of the 'macrocosm' that makes up our record of the world of knowledge. The compiler of a bibliography will need to be aware of the other forms: library catalogues; current national bibliographies; indexes and abstracting services, mostly for recent periodical and related texts; those guides, indexes, calendars and other lists that cover archival collections; scholarly descriptive bibliographies; and bibliographical essays. These bibliographical forms may be accessible in books, on cards or as computer data bases; they may be assembled locally, co-operatively or through the so-called 'bibliographical utilities'. The compiler of a bibliography will use their contents and will come to know their practices, procedures and policy decisions—typically more painstaking and ostensibly more logical than the compiler's own, although likely to be more rigid than he or she will need to be encumbered with—as well as their resulting idiosyncrasies. But if the compiler's efforts are to have any intellectual legitimacy, the conception of the bibliography will be different from those of the other forms.

The compiler's world is likely to be more limited, if not always in breadth of subject, at least in the number of items involved and by the self-contained nature of the product. Library catalogue departments need to devise practices that will allow for new books, indexing programs for anticipating their next periodical publication, and data bases for accommodating new entries on a continuous basis; but all good compilers at best will envisage a supplement, a second edition, or some kind of sequel. Compilers of bibliographies are privileged to be able to count to the day when they can say, 'this bibliography is now complete—so far as I am concerned'. This finality is the basis for freedoms the compiler should use to enhance the presentation of the bibliography.

Recalling the thousands of bibliographies that have been compiled, we might ask whether a manual for compilers is really needed. There may be few writings on the subject, and little concern for modeling, for good reason: the method is common sense and basically self-obvious, a matter of matching resources to special needs. 'There is little to teach,' one observer has noted, 'if much to learn.'[1] Isn't a manual on this topic as pretentious as one for telling the time or riding a bicycle, as hopeless as a textbook on how to compose a symphony or paint a masterpiece? Isn't the range of bibliographies—from casual one-page reading lists to the lifetime achievements of Friedrich Adolf Ebert, Samuel Austin Allibone and Charles Evans; from popular readings on nuclear energy, to Renaissance descriptions of French cathedrals for scholars, to early Benton Harbor imprints—simply too vast to justify any useful generalizations?

There are two answers. First, any compiler will benefit from seeing the total process in perspective. By describing the steps and suggesting the options, this book may help avoid some false starts. Secondly, seeing the whole picture of the work to be done should encourage and engage more than it intimidates. Bibliographical work being at once fascinating, meticulously absorbing, and open-ended, some direction is particularly needed for those who embark on extended projects with a view to publication or some other final product in mind.

Meanwhile, the vast improvements in access to bibliographical references have inevitably led to visionary hopes and dreams, to threats and predictions that bibliographies will become obsolete in deference to larger and more aggressive and utopian members of the bibliographical macrocosm, or that their compilation might be achieved by pushing a button (what John Metcalfe probably had in mind in his term, 'panaceatic bibliography'. [2] The compiler's task is, in practice, highly labour intensive. Assuming that excellence calls for the capacity for taking appropriate pains, the object of this study may be seen as one of identifying and defending those pains. It must thus at once address both the aspiring compiler and the student of bibliographical policy: the former by suggesting matters of justification, the latter by looking closely at matters of practice.

WRITINGS ON THE COMPILING OF BIBLIOGRAPHIES. Among the very few manuals for compilers, Marion Villiers Higgins, *Bibliography: A Beginner's Guide to Making, Evaluation, and Use of Bibliographies* (New York: H. W. Wilson, 1941) remains the standard brief, practical and general source. Georg Schneider's essay, comprising the 'Theoretisch-Geschichtlicher Teil' in the early editions of his *Handbuch der Bibliographie* (Leipzig: Hiersemann, 1923), pp. 3–199, and translated by Ralph Shaw as *Theory and History of Bibliography* (New York: Columbia University Press, 1934), includes many of the major perspectives presented in this book. More practical in its objectives, and more recent, is A. M. Lewin Robinson, *Systematic Bibliography: A Practical Guide to the Work of Compilation* (1963: 4th ed., London: Clive Bingley; Munich, New York, Paris: K. G. Saur, 1979).

Other writings on the compiling of bibliographies are cited in the 'Bibliography'. Hereinafter all works listed there are cited in short form, both in the documentary references at the ends of the chapters and in the bibliographical notes within the chapters.

In overview, this literature may usefully be grouped under the following rubrics. First, writings that mainly address procedural and technical problems in general, notably Cole (1901), Schrero (1930), Shaw (1954 and 1964), Hodgson (1957), Bryant and Iyengar (both 1960) and Kumar (1976) among them. Second, writings conceived for purposes of training librarians, Van Hoesen and Walter (1928) and Wynar (1963) among them, with Hackman (1970) addressing bibliographical searching activities in particular. Third, the writings that address subject disciplines and their peculiarities: widely divergent in their approaches but all admirable in their concerns, these writings range from Staveley and the McIlwaines (1970) and Davinson (1975) again addressing the aspiring librarian, Bourton

(1967) with practical advice, to Hale (1970) and Batts (1978) specifically concerned with subject literatures.

The literature of bibliographical compilation also extends into the area of technical writing manuals, some of which have excellent if very brief sections on how to compile bibliographies, others of which explore interesting peripheries that may be helpful. This literature is set forth in three complementary lists: Russell Shank, *Bibliography of Technical Writing* (2nd ed., Columbus, Ohio: Society of Technical Writers and Editors, New York Chapter, 1958); Theresa Ammannito Philler, Ruth K. Hersch, and Helen V. Carlson, *An Annotated Bibliography of Technical Writing, Editing, Graphics, and Publishing, 1950–1965* (Washington, D.C.: Society of Technical Writers and Publishers; Pittsburgh: Carnegie Library of Pittsburgh, 1965); and Gerald J. Alred, Diana C. Reep, and Mohan R. Limaye, *Business and Technical Writing: Annotated Bibliography of Books, 1880–1980* (Metuchen, N.J.: Scarecrow Press, 1981). James R. Frakes, 'Forms, Measured Forms . . .', *College English*, 22 (1960–61), 213–17, is also valuable for its evaluative viewpoints. As an example of a technical writing manual that is well conceived in addressing the compiler, I would cite John H. Mitchell, *Writing for Professional and Technical Journals* (New York: John Wiley, 1968), chapters 2–3, pp. 9–88.

BIBLIOGRAPHY IN GENERAL

The term bibliography can have two definitions: there is bibliography itself, an activity, and there is *a* bibliography, the product of this activity. Bibliographies generally belong to two groups, one concerned with the listing of books and other documents, the other concerned primarily with the study of books as physical objects. The first group, which is the better known, is commonly seen as a Germanic line. It extends from the practical grass roots approach of the present book, to the highly technical fields of modern documentation and information science. It includes two specialities called *systematic* and *enumerative* bibliography. The two are interrelated if not virtually synonymous. Some writers have proposed that the systematic bibliographer studies the way of compiling lists while the enumerative bibliographer studies the use of lists. If the two must be distinguished at all, this distinction would be one way to do it.

The second group is concerned with the study of books as physical objects. Historically it has been mostly an English line, extending to the study of literary criticism in terms of book production; the French presence is now coming to be recognized, in a special concern for the book as a cultural force. The several overlapping specialities in this side of the field include *analytical* bibliography, concerned with the ways in which specific books as physical objects were produced; *textual* bibliography, which uses these findings in the important work of establishing authenticity of content; and *historical* bibliography, which considers the relationships between a civilization and its books.

While the two groups of bibliography and their specialities can be seen advantageously as independent activities, they must also usefully come together. They do so most conspicuously in *descriptive* bibliography, concerned with the specification of particulars, based on the methods of analytical bibliography, and with addressing the 'history of the forms in which a given group of books was presented to the public'. [3] The notion that the first group of bibliography is 'applied', and the second 'pure', is fascinating, but hard to sustain logically. It does, however, tell us much about the values and goals of the major practitioners through history.

WRITINGS ON THE DEFINITION OF BIBLIOGRAPHY. Among the numerous discussions that attempt to define bibliography, *see* Freer (1954), Hibberd (1965), Stokes (the 1967 and 1969 books), Blum (1969) and Tanselle (1974). The articles on bibliography in major encyclopaedias also provide useful brief overviews of the several domains of bibliography. Among these Grand (1888), Pollard (1910), Clapp (1957), Stokes (1969) and Francis (1976) are probably most notable. For an interesting perspective directed mostly toward descriptive bibliography, *see* Ross Atkinson, 'An Application of Semiotics to the Definition of Bibliography,' *Studies in Bibliography*, 33 (1980), 54–73.

THE NEED FOR BIBLIOGRAPHIES

The 'information explosion' has no doubt been going on since Adam and Eve; we hope and pray it will never stop. More is being written; and there are more forms of recorded knowledge — printed ephemera, works in new media, unpublished materials which, thanks to the camera, we now need to consider as never before. Furthermore, our libraries are improving their resources and services, so that we rarely can be excused for ignoring important material of any kind.

It is an exaggeration to propose that the problem of learning today is one of 'graphomania'[4] —publish or perish, everyone writes and no one reads, everyone talks and no one listens; perhaps better to ask, when was it otherwise? Today's fortunate reader certainly has a better selection than any in the past and needs more than ever to be led in the right direction. The writer also has a bigger job of finding who might previously have covered his subject. Both the simple attractiveness and the mischievous ignorance in the view that 'the problem of bibliographical organization is a matter of how little to read' is readily apparent.[5]

The need to organize this expanding world of recorded knowledge becomes all the greater and all the more impossible. As our library catalogues grow older, larger and perhaps more refined, they also become more cumbersome, more limited in their coverage and more subject to varying interpretations of their rules. Older writings are rarely re-catalogued to meet new needs, while detailed subject analysis of contents was long ago deferred to other bibliographical enterprises, among them enumerative bibliographies.

WRITINGS ON BIBLIOGRAPHICAL CONTROL. The major study, and the source for the concept of macrocosm and microcosm, is Shera and Egan (1950). Their efforts have many predecessors, among them Campbell (1896) and Josephson (1912). The impact of the 1950 report has been both wide and deep; among the varied offspring, see Dunkin and Ranganathan (both 1953), Boehm (1965 and 1972), Wilson (1968), Simon (1973), Anderson and Mangouni (both 1974), Davinson (1975), the 1976 Chicago conference, Hickey (1978) and, among the most thoughtful syntheses, B. C. Brookes, 'Jesse Shera and the Theory of Bibliography', *Journal of Librarianship*, 5 (1973), 233–45.

THE HISTORY OF BIBLIOGRAPHY

The earliest bibliography, however defined, is lost in the dawn of historical records. It perhaps coincided with the origins of research in the time of Aristotle, blending scholarly exposition with the identification of relevant evidence. This was also the characteristic of several medieval, Byzantine and Moslem texts that function both as exposition and bibliography. Lists from the late Middle Ages were mostly inventories of particular collections; only with the Renaissance and the advent of printing do we find lists conceived mostly for the purpose of defining the literature of particular topics: Champier (1506) on medicine and Nevizzano (1522) on law, Erasmus of Rotterdam (1523) on a single author (himself), Bale (1548) and Doni (1551) on national literatures, and Gesner (1545–55) with a monumental universal bibliography indexed by subject. By the next century the first bibliography of bibliographies was compiled (Labbé, 1664). This period also saw the first learned scientific journals, and the first of the *Acta*, glorifying and criticizing the achievement of men of learning before their peers.

By the nineteenth century the need for macrocosmic planning was becoming evident, leading to vast special indexes to learned and periodical literature such as those compiled under the auspices of the Royal Society in London and by William F. Poole and his successors in North America, and to the visionary plan of the International Institute of Bibliography in Brussels. The time was also ripe for even more bibliographies of bibliographies, guides to bibliographies, bibliographies of the guides, and guides to the guides. Our last great bibliography of bibliographies, by Theodore Besterman, contained over 117,000 entries; and this total consisted only of separately issued lists—*not* those issued in periodicals or other series, or as compilations at the end of a book—and published before 1963! The *Bibliographic Index* and other similar guides cite several thousand new lists each year, but all of them on a highly selective basis. (These and other major guides to bibliographies are cited at the end of this chapter.) Our only bibliography of bibliographies of bibliographies was compiled seventy to eighty years ago,[6] a fact that has to be seen as evidence of how many levels of abstraction the human mind finds usefully imposed on reality. In any event, the compiler's faith often must resemble that of the tortoise racing Achilles, backwards. Bibliographies, of course, must be continuing to appear because they are continuing to be used; and in fact, employing the classic survey question and asking a sample of particular readers which of the various kinds of bibliographical records they most recently consulted, bibliographical lists no doubt would claim a handsome proportion of the total.

WRITINGS ON THE HISTORY OF BIBLIOGRAPHY. The best surveys are still Grand (1888) and Schneider (1923), as well as Fritz Homeyer, 'Versuch eines Bibliographen-Lexikons', in *Bibliographie und Buchhandel: Festschrift zur Einweihung des Neubaus der Deutschen Bibliothek* (Frankfurt am Main: Börsenverein des deutschen Buchhandels, 1959), pp. 141–63. The major recent scholar has been Archer Taylor, whose perspectives are scattered through his *Renaissance Guides to Books* (Berkeley, Los Angeles: University of California Press, 1945), *A History of Bibliographies of Bibliographies* (New Brunswick, N.J.: Scarecrow Press, 1955), *Book Catalogues: Their Varieties and Uses* (Chicago: Newberry Library, 1957), *Catalogues of Rare Books: A Chapter in Bibliographical History* (Lawrence: University of Kansas Libraries, 1958) and *General Subject-Indexes since 1548* (Philadelphia: University of Pennsylvania Press, 1966). The early period has been surveyed in Lester Condit, 'Bibliography in its Prenatal Existence', *Library Quarterly*, 7 (1937), 564–76; John Webster Spargo, 'Some Reference Books of the 16th and 17th Centuries', *Papers of the Bibliographical Society of America*, 31 (1937), 133–75; and Theodore Besterman, *The Beginnings of Systematic Bibliography* (London: Oxford University Press, 1935; 2nd ed., 1936), but preferably in the 3rd ed. of this work, published as *Les débuts de la bibliographie méthodique* (Paris: La Palme, 1950). For a history of work at the national level, *see* Katherine O. Murra, 'Notes on the Development of the Concept of Current Complete National Bibliography', issued as an appendix to *Bibliographical Services: Their Present State and Possibilities for Future Improvement* ('The Unesco/Library of Congress Bibliographical Survey'; Washington, 1950); Rudolf Blum, 'Vor- und frühgeschichte der nationalen Allgemeinbibliographie', *Archiv für Geschichte des Buchwesens*, 2 (1959), 233–303; and LeRoy H. Linder, *The Rise of Current Complete National Bibliography* (New York: Scarecrow Press, 1959). The history of cataloguing practice is summarized in Gertrude London (1980), which reorganizes and updates some of the major points of Dorothy Mae Norris, *A History of Cataloguing and Cataloguing Methods, 1100–1850* (London: Grafton, 1939). David Foxon, *Thoughts on the History and Future of*

Bibliographical Description (Berkeley: University of California, School of Librarianship; Los Angeles: School of Library Science, 1970), provocatively surveys the context of descriptive bibliography. Batts (1978) is concerned with events in the German-speaking world, while British bibliographical history includes, among the notable works, Sears R. Jayne, *Library Catalogues of the English Renaissance* (Berkeley: University of California Press, 1956) and W. Boyd Rayward, *Systematic Bibliography in England, 1850–1895* (Urbana: University of Illinois, Graduate School of Library Science, 1967; Occasional papers, 84). The work of booksellers in particular is treated in Graham Pollard and A. Ehrman, *The Distribution of Books by Catalogue from the Invention of Printing to A.D. 1800* (Cambridge: Printed for . . . the Roxburghe Club, 1965).

The task of compiling lists thus becomes more than a diverting and enlightening pastime. It is also a responsibility growing out of our belief in the value of providing access to information. Any text that is significant and substantial enough to be published ought to be known about so that it can be consulted. The premise may be debated with any number of specific instances in mind, but in principle it is virtually an article of faith in a free society. A text that is not discoverable, like the one that is not available, for all practical purposes does not exist. The compiling of bibliographies implies an active opposition to censorship, related to our faith in the importance of human diversity. Yet the task of the bibliographer may appear to be a form of censorship in its own right (Ortega calls it 'mastering the raging book'). [7] The task needs to be seen with Francis Bacon's euphoric optimism:

The multitude of books produces a deceitful impression of superfluity. This, however, is not to be remedied by destroying the books already written, but by making more good ones, which like the serpent of Moses, may devour serpents of the enchanters. [8]

And as bibliographies continue to appear and be used, libraries acquire them liberally. Furthermore, they probably do so with lower standards than they apply to printed texts themselves—a situation that may be understandable but is none the less unfortunate. In evaluating bibliographies, the time-honoured

adjective is 'useful', in much the same sense that modern art works
are described as 'interesting'.

THE NATURE OF
BIBLIOGRAPHICAL WORK

A widespread notion has it that compiling bibliographies lacks
intellectual dignity. One remembers Sir Walter Greg's observation that 'it is convenient to students of any subject to regard
bibliographers as a race of useful drudges—*servi a bibliotheca*—who
are there to do for them some of the spade-work they are too lazy
or too incompetent to do for themselves.'[9] Or Herman Melville's
address to the 'mere painstaking burrower grubworm of a poor
devil of a Sub-sub-librarian,' who, in search of references to
whales,

> appears to have gone through the long Vaticans and street-stalls
> of the earth . . . . Thou belongest to that hopeless, sallow tribe
> which no wine of this world will ever warm; . . . but with
> whom one sometimes loves to sit, and feel poor-devilish, too;
> and grow convivial upon tears.[10]

It is not only possible but very easy for the compiler's work to
consist entirely of burrowing. The burrowing becomes seductive,
even exciting, when unexpected things turn up, as they so often
do. If not already an expert in the field, the compiler often becomes
admirably learned in the subject. But bibliographical work can
also be done without any original contribution being intended or
made—an activity best viewed as a 'handmaiden' service to the
work of others, an 'auxilliary science', or as the Germans would
have it, a *Hilfswissenschaft*. Practitioners maybe committed to a
'second-class citizenship' in the world of learning, but this is not to
disparage either the value of such labours to scholarship or their
powers of diversion.

It frequently happens that the compiler is led out of routine facts
into scholarship itself. This happy development may arise from

natural curiosity to learn more about one's discoveries. It can also result when the list calls for critical annotations, or when a topic demands a complete re-organization, the old systems having become obsolete or awkward. One of the most impressive of all bibliographies, if it could ever be assembled, would consist of the major contributions to knowledge that have grown out of 'routine' compilations. With this in mind, the compiler who views the task as an altogether casual effort may wish to pin up this pronouncement from George Watson Cole: 'Every bibliographer, while making his investigations, should pursue them as if at some time he intended to write a comprehensive work upon the subject of his labors.'[11] Jackson Bryer grumbles that 'the enumerative bibliographer is probably also the greatest appreciator of good scholarship because only he has waded through so much murky water to get to it.'[12] It is difficult to disagree with John Ferguson's observation that the bibliographer's 'equipment consists of patience, care, accuracy, a constant lookout for the books wanted, and a persistent determination to apply these qualities to research';[13] and it is difficult to argue that he is not also specifying some of the attributes of good scholars of all kinds.

The self-obvious distinction between a prose text and a bibliography is one of medium of presentation. One uses sentences, the other citations. But beneath lies the question of the appropriateness of either to its objectives. Originality has nothing necessarily to do with the matter: there are prose texts that derive simply from other prose texts, and there are bibliographies that make original contributions either in overall conception or details. The prose text organizes the answers while the bibliography indicates where to find the answers. But this begs a larger question. In the prose text the statements are processed, incorporated into a definitive and original form through the exercise of logic and rhetoric, so as to be, if not final, at least sufficient to the author's conception of the reader's needs; the bibliography assumes that the reader will want and be willing to look for his own finality or sufficiency through a commitment of further time and effort. While less fully consummated intellectually, the bibliography may be the more hopeful, the more evangelical statement. At the same time it would be absurd not to concede that the bibliography clearly lacks the possibilities for reasoning that make for powerful intellectual statements.

Jean Meyriat's definition of the bibliographer, 'a specialist who is willing to give up much of his time to analyzing the thoughts of others instead of thinking for himself',[14] may therefore seem ennobling in its modesty. Individual compilers might even be forgiven for accepting a demeaning or 'below stairs' status in so far as it can give a sense of security in the bustling world of intellectual commerce and some of the pride that comes from conspicuous humility. After all, scholars in subject areas do need help with their literature searches and can hardly be blamed for endorsing this position for anyone willing to espouse it. But for the servitude to be justified on grounds that no intellectual activity is involved is another matter, and Appendix B should be useful as a response to it, based on the text that follows. The wrongness of Meyriat's attitude and its deleterious effects could, in fact, be part of the reason for the paucity of previous writings on the subject.

Whatever the aspirations, the bibliographer needs, as Stanley Pargellis once put it, an equal mixture of discrimination and imagination.[15] It is hard to say very much about the imagination, which is variable and unpredictable, depending on the right compiler finding the right insights at the right time. But the discrimination has to be viewed as a combination of discipline and flexibility. So far the methods for compiling a bibliography seem largely to reflect the classic taunt associated with elite institutions: 'there aren't any rules until you've broken one of them.' This book is essentially an attempt to organize the rules in their judgemental more than their mechanical contexts. By exploring the reasons behind the rules, the compiler should be better able to consider the needs to break or adjust the rules in the cause of a more effective presentation. Such flexibility, addressed to the particular needs of specialized readers, has to be seen as a major justification for our continued work with and creation of bibliographies.

NOTES

1. Wilson, *Two Kinds of Power* (1968), p, 56n.
2. Cited in W. Boyd Rayward, *Systematic Bibliography in England, 1850–1895* (Urbana: University of Illinois, Graduate School of Library Science, 1967: Occasional Papers, 84), p. 6.
3. G. Thomas Tanselle, 'Some Remarks on Bibliographical Nonproliferation,' *Proof*, 1 (1971), 174–5.
4. Milan Kundera, *The Book of Laughter and Forgetting* (New York: Alfred A. Knopf, 1980; London: Faber, 1982), pp. 91–2.
5. D. J. Urquhart, quoted in Jesse H. Shera, *Libraries and the Organization of Knowledge* (Hamden, Conn.: Archon Books, 1965), p. 107.
6. Aksel G. S. Josephson, *Bibliographies of Bibliographies Chronologically Arranged* (Chicago: Bibliographical Society of Chicago, 1901: Contributions to Bibliography, 1), and expanded in *Papers of the Bibliographical Society of America*, 2 (1910), 21–4, 54–6; 3 (1911), 23–4, 50–3; 4 (1912), 23–7; and 7 (1912–13), 115–24.
7. José Ortega y Gasset, 'The Mission of the Librarian,' translated by James Lewis and Ray L. Carpenter, *Antioch Review*, 21 (1961), 151.
8. *The Advancement of Learning* (New York: Colonial Press, 1900), p. 44.
9. W. W. Greg, 'Bibliography: A Retrospect', in *The Bibliographical Society, 1892–1942: Studies in Retrospect* (London: Bibliographical Society, 1945), p. 24.
10. In the preliminary statement of 'Extracts' in *Moby Dick* (Berkeley, Los Angeles, London: University of California Press, 1979), p. ix.
11. Cole, 'Compiling a Bibliography' (1901), p. 792.
12. Bryer, 'From Second-Class Citizenship' (1978), pp. 55–61.
13. Ferguson, *Some Aspects* (1900), p. 29.
14. *Report of the General Principles concerning International Bibliographical Work* (Paris: UNESCO, 1957; UNESCO/CUA/82), p. 13.
15. Stanley Pargellis, 'Gesner, Petzoldt, et al,' *Papers of the Bibliographical Society of America*, 53 (1959), 20.

SUPPLEMENT TO CHAPTER I

Major Guides to Bibliographies

Bibliographies may be indispensable to scholarship; but, sad to report, their vast world itself is under very poor bibliographical control. General guides, intended primarily for library reference use, have been prepared along national lines. Walford (English), Sheehy (American), the venerable Malclès (French), and Arnold, as well as Totok and Weitzel (both German, the latter covering bibliographies only), all largely duplicate each other, but are sometimes complementary as a result of their somewhat different conceptions of scope and readership. Collison surveys some of this same area, in a prose discussion that brings out relationships that a list would forego. Davinson's *Bibliographic Control* (1975) is also valuable for its prose context.

For more exhaustive coverage of the world of bibliographies, the definitive but dated list is Besterman. His predecessors are cited in columns 782–842 of the 4th ed. A continuation, such as Besterman himself insisted was impossible, is now being undertaken at the Library of Congress, the Toomey list being the first cumulation of this activity. Besterman's arrangement is by subject; Arnim provides the counterpart listing for individual names. Besterman, furthermore, is limited to monographic publications; the lists published as parts of other books or journals have never been collected universally, although several current indexes provide some coverage of newly published lists. The *Bibliographic Index* describes new titles of special interest in public and general libraries; *Bibliographische Berichte* attempts much the same for scholarly literature; while the *Bulletin of Bibliography* includes timely reference lists, many of them in the belles lettres. The on-line *Directory* is one of several guides to the various kinds of sources (bibliographical, numerical) available in the United States, in an area of growing bibliographical importance and sophistication.

Such current lists may be necessarily general in their coverage, but they will also direct compilers to the major specialist services and lists. The two Gray books, now somewhat dated, also provide valuable access to the current guides used by specialists in particular subject disciplines.

Arnim, Max. *Internationale Personalbibliographie.* 2nd ed. Leipzig, Stuttgart: Hiersemann, 1944–50; a continuation by Gerhard Bock and Franz Hodes is in progress, 1963– .

Arnold, Robert F. *Allgemeine Bücherkunde zur neueren deutschen Literaturgeschichte.* 4th ed. Berlin: Walter de Gruyter, 1966.

Besterman, Theodore. *World Bibliography of Bibliographies.* 4th ed. Lausanne: Societas Bibliographica, 1965.

Bibliographic Index: A Cumulative Bibliography of Bibliographies. New York: H. W. Wilson, 1938– .

Bibliographie der deutschen Bibliographien. Leipzig: VEB Verlag für Buch- und Bibliothekswesen, 1957– .

Bibliographische Berichte. Frankfurt: Klostermann, 1959– .

Bohatta, Hanns, and Franz Hodes. *Internationale Bibliographie der Bibliographien.* Frankfurt: Klostermann, 1950.

Bulletin of Bibliography. Boston: F. W. Faxon; Westport, Conn.: Meckler, 1897– .

Collison, Robert L. *Bibliographies, Subject and National.* 3rd ed. London: Crosby Lockwood, 1968.

Directory of On-Line Databases. Santa Monica, Cal.: Cuadra Associates, 1979– .

Gray, Richard A. *A Guide to Book Review Citations.* Columbus, Ohio: Ohio State University Press, 1968.

————. *Serial Bibliographies in the Humanities and Social Sciences.* Ann Arbor: Pierian Press, 1969.

Malclès, Louise-Noëlle. *Les sources du travail bibliographique.* Geneva: E. Droz; Lille: Girard, 1950–8.

Sheehy, Eugene P. (former editions by Alice Bertha Kroeger, Isadore Gilbert Mudge, and Constance M. Winchell). *Guide to Reference Books.* 9th ed. Chicago: American Library Association, 1976; supplements in progress, 1980– .

Toomey, Alice F. *A World Bibliography of Bibliographies, 1964–1974: A List of Works represented by Library of Congress Printed Catalog Cards; A Decennial Supplement to . . . Besterman . . . .* Totowa, N.J.: Rowman & Littlefield, 1977.

Totok, Wilhelm, Karl-Heinz Weimann, & Rolf Weitzel. *Handbuch der bibliographischen Nachschlagewerke.* 4th ed. Frankfurt: Klostermann, 1972.

Walford, A. J. *Guide to Reference Materials.* 3rd ed. London: The Library Association, 1973–77; 4th ed. in progress, 1980– .

CHAPTER II

Scope

TOPICS

The range of topics for bibliographies is unlimited. Old ones need to be re-examined every few years, or every generation, or every two centuries. Often a supplement to a standard work is needed. Entirely new topics also call out for attention, frequently emerging from the special infatuations of imaginative compilers. Topics may reflect the interests of the compiler, or they may be assigned by an outside agency. 'Avoid highly innocent topics drawn from hobbies which are intended to relax rather than to excite the mind,'[1] advises one writer. Many valuable lists were probably prepared by partly or wholly apathetic or antipathetic compilers, just as there are many estimable and indispensable lists that appear to have served no obvious immediate needs when they were compiled. Often a formal bibliography will grow out of an informal literature survey.

WRITINGS ON TOPIC SELECTION AND DEFINITION. The literature devoted to the selection and definition of a compiler's topic is sketchy indeed. In the literature on compilation, Schneider (in the 1934 translation), pp. 78–89, and Staveley and the McIlwaines (1967), pp. 11–25 (Chapter 1: 'Areas of Subject Study') address the question in context, while Bercaw (1956), Bourton (1959) and Walford (1960) make valuable observations based on their experience. One must look further afield for the best discussions.

Among them is Kenneth W. Houp and Thomas E. Pearsall, *Reporting Technical Information* (3rd ed., Beverly Hills, Calif.: Glencoe Press, 1967), pp. 36–59 (Chapter 3: 'Gathering Information') and 60–77 (Chapter 4: 'Analyzing your Audience'). Other brief discussions of import include Jacques Barzun and Henry F. Graff, *The Modern Researcher* (3rd ed., New York: Harcourt Brace Jovanovich, 1977), esp. pp. 15–18; Mary Travis Arny and Christopher R. Reaske, *Ecology: A Writer's Handbook* (New York: Random House, 1972), esp. pp. 13–18 (Chapter 2: 'Selecting the Topic') and 21–9 (Chapter 3: 'Restricting and Developing the Topic'); Jacqueline M. Morris and Elizabeth A. Elkins, *Library Searching: Resources and Strategies, with Examples from the Environmental Sciences* (New York: Jeffrey Norton, 1978), pp. 81–5 (Chapter 9: 'The Bibliography'), and *passim.*; and Knud Larsen, *On the Teaching of Bibliography, with a Survey of its Aims and Methods* (Copenhagen: Royal School of Librarianship, 1961).

Topics of today, the fashionable or timely topics, have a number of assets and deserve a special word. They are likely to be in demand, so as to be appealing to publishers. But they also call for brave and imaginative compilers, willing to confront formidable obstacles. For instance, the writings will be new and not likely to be well covered in other bibliographical lists. They will likely be found in a variety of bibliographical forms: journals, leaflets, reports, newspaper articles, journal articles, taped interviews in archival repositories. Library acquisitions and processing programmes are still notoriously slow for many of these kinds of materials, requiring the compiler to depend on various personal and special repositories. The documents are also likely to be hard to cite with any consistency. The newness of the topic makes both definition and bibliographical organization difficult: the compiler is likely to be too close to the topic to see its appropriate structure and its internal interrelationships. Finally, even more so than with other bibliographies, the list will stand a high chance of becoming obsolete: if the topic continues to be popular something better will come along, possibly based on the compiler's work, and if the topic declines the work will be forgotten. These are points to be taken into consideration, not reasons for doing nothing.

At the other extreme are topics that may look dead but really are only dormant. Perhaps nobody has looked at them for years because nothing more needs to be said; but the time may be right for a redefinition of the topic, a new organization of the content, or a new evaluation of the writings. Since often as not the literature is ample and intimidating, the redefinition may appropriately fall to a compiler well versed in the history of the subject. Antiquarian booksellers in particular enjoy telling how fields of scholarship have been opened, and re-opened, thanks to the appearance of a bibliography. The imaginative compiler, in any event, enters a field barren of activity or fertile, convinced that he or she can contribute to it.

LITERATURES AND READERS

The compiler's commitment to the topic is essentially an act of faith. However dispassionate he or she is in executing the tasks and however cruel in evaluating the authors, the goal is the greater glory of the topic. Compilers can even rightly be carried away to the point of viewing their faith as essentially trinitarian, believing that there are materials that need to be noticed, that there are people who want and need to know about them, and that their efforts can help to bring the two together. Such an intermediary role helps to force the compiler to be particularly aware of the literature and its characteristics and to surmise about readers and their characteristics.

Dr Johnson distinguished between the books in Mr Cambridge's library and the backs of those books: the subject and its literature, however interdependent, are two different things. Most specialists are too busy to remember exactly where they learned all they know about their subject; and there are indispensable bibliographers and librarians who know the sources very well but the substance only superficially. The state of knowledge redefines itself through its literature: the dynamics of a field is governed in large part—and arguably ought to be governed entirely—by the reactions to evidence that is formally presented in its documents.

For each of the various fields of learning there are distinctive presentations—distinctive conceptions of truth, styles of prose, forms of etiquette, lengths of text, modes of publishing and critical institutions for judging excellence. Some depend mostly on periodical articles, others on government documents, others on report literature, still others on trade books. Following the Battle of the Books around 1700, some literatures fall into the humanistic pattern that recommends the original and earliest statement as the best, while others fall into the scientific pattern that defers to the newest. And there are differing notions of the basic distinction between 'primary' and 'secondary' sources. Some subject fields are 'hard', self-consciously 'scientific' and governed by rigid methodologies of testing and proof, while others are 'soft', looking mostly for important, interesting and relevant insights that are attractive if not political. Sometimes there are surprising and less than subtle national differences. Bourton, for instance, tells of how she discovered that the British patent literature on gauge control of strip rolling mills was concerned mostly with control devices, the American more with factors affecting gauge control;[2] the national patterns in fields like sociology and cultural history, of course, have filled entire books. Some fields are heavily documented in their scholarship, and others are not; some prefer that foreign-language statements be translated, while others prefer the original. Some allow for casual observations, even humour in their prose. Some flourish on statistical tables or other approaches to objectivity, even at times on sheer and intimidating pedantry. Most are based in academic disciplines that preach interdisciplinary co-operation but usually growl fiercely, and ineffectively, at poachers. The compiler must be sensitive to such matters if he is to achieve the fullest comprehension of the literature or literatures to which his topic most clearly belongs.

Every subject has not only its characteristic literature, but also its characteristic network of bibliographical coverage—a 'mesocosm' of sorts between microcosm and macrocosm—which the compiler must come to know thoroughly. Some subject areas, definable broadly or narrowly, can depend on single definitive and monumental retrospective lists for either primary or secondary sources or both; others call on a variety of lists often because the materials themselves defy unification. Most areas have gaps which are embarrassing more in theory than in practice; perhaps no one has really cared enough about the gap to bother to fill it. Some have dependable and regularly updated current services that call attention to new writings, while others rely on a variety of newsletters, grapevines, publishers' announcements, and the like. Some serve specialists very well but general readers badly, conservative interests well but adventuresome ones badly, or vice versa. Some areas can depend largely on the *National Union Catalog*, the *Education Index*, or other extensive current services, while some call for bibliographical works in adjacent subject areas. The compiler must know or expect to learn all of the lists in question, both for collecting and working with his own entries and for justifying his own topic as part of a bibliographical network. There is of course no point in doing what someone has already done well, but there can be every reason for doing again what others have done incompletely or badly. In even the most densely covered areas, however, there always seems to be room for new lists which at the very least will be credited as 'useful', or at best will open important perspectives for an audience of readers.

The literature consists of documents created in the past; the readers can only be guessed at, since they will exist in the future. [3] Identifying them is an exercise in optimism, based on vague principles. There are different levels of specialization characterized by students or amateurs as distinguished from advanced research scholars, psychologists as distinct from historians, or Italian historians as distinct from European or even Florentine historians. Decisions in identifying the readership are manifest in a multitude of ways: in scope; in choice of titles (foreign-language texts or early writings, as opposed to popularizations and review); in arrangement (chronological or alphabetical, or in small or large subject categories); in the nature and vocabulary of the annotations; in the presence or absence of particular features, such as addresses of obscure publishers for current library acquisitions; or in what the compiler chooses to index.

The compiler defines an audience as those who will be able to use the list more comfortably than others. He will always work to reach as broad an audience as possible, somewhat in keeping with Barzun's proposal that 'the reportmaker must write always as if addressing the whole educated community'. [4] But he can never do so without a certain discomfort, since he will be asking some of his readers to work at levels or in areas of specialization other than those they are trained to handle conveniently.

The decisions in identifying and delimiting readers are essentially negative, and hence can be brutally quick. In contrast, the decisions to help those readers are more positive, painstaking and continuing, calling as they do for the compiler's thoughtfulness and helpfulness. Readers will be looking for specific texts they ought to know about and for general impressions of the literature on the subject. In both quests, they will be helped by a rather magical characteristic of some bibliographies, which enables particular statements virtually to leap out to the reader's attention. Such sorcery is of course an exaggeration. At best there are pages that can be easily scanned, and on them a crucial word or number readily spotted. At worst there are those miserable reference works, many of them older and German, in small and crabbed type, badly leaded, that require the reader to proceed line by line, word by word, guided by the index finger. Good design of entries with visual mobility in mind is obviously crucial. Other amenities will likely include the right introduction and overview of the contents, running heads or other devices on each page to enable readers to find their way, and appropriate indexes, well laid out. Only by analyzing their own experiences as users of bibliographies, can compilers become aware of the opportunities for their lists to become—to use the term now popular with cataloguers and computer systems specialists—'user-friendly'.

ADOPTING AND ADAPTING

How much should compilers 'tailor' their presentation to the peculiarities of their chosen literature and its readers? Should the concerns of the microcosm be allowed to overrule those of the macrocosm? Such questions will underlie many of the compiler's basic decisions, in matters of scope, arrangement, layout, special features, and, above all, citation style.

It will be particularly convenient if a compiler can simply adopt well-defined practices, whether modeled on our venerable bibliographies (i.e., CBEL, or Walford or Sheehy) or vast abstracting services (i.e., *Biological Abstracts*, or one of the INSPEC services), or as set forth in one of the various codes for library cataloguing. The compiler is thus spared the considerable anguish of improvising rules and practices, and the result will make convenient sense to anyone who knows the model. In a sense, this present book—as it collects and organizes the perspectives of past practices, praises their virtues and questions their faults, and in general seeks to define the ideal bibliography—addresses this very issue.

The manifest historical trend, probably dating from the advent of the printing press but seen most notably over the past hundred years, has moved in the direction of uniform practices. The recent events of course will coincide with the rise of modern librarianship, and its cataloguing codes in particular. Significantly, they also reflect on intellectual and social trends vaguely associated with what is known as the Whig interpretation of history: an appeal to the cause of benefiting the needs of the general citizenry of enlightened and deserving nations, a deep faith that these honourable causes were 'progressive', and thus an assurance that other long-term historical trends were working on behalf of their efforts. This faith can clearly claim a major role in the development of our bibliographical systems, and in the improvement in bibliographical control in our century. Questioning such progress is rightly damned as reactionary: the alternative to bibliographical uniformity is a bibliographical Babel.

As the fuller dimensions of the history of bibliography may some day come to be uncovered, of course, we may find that the long-term trend is not necessarily toward uniformity at all. The bibliographical record has demonstrably become more extensive and more comprehensive over the past century; but the larger world of bibliographical references has also expanded, creating a growing *demimonde* of documentary footnotes, orally transmitted citations, library acquisitions formulae, and reference algorithms.[5] Furthermore, we can even now see how some of our cherished bibliographical institutions—our outmoded universal classification schemes, as an example—after a time run their course, and become more of a liability than a good thing. Whether the forces toward uniformity are the 'right' ones, furthermore, is beside the point here, since the compiler's main task is not one of advancing long-term Whiggish ideals but of serving a delimited audience of specialist readers. If standardized practices come to be accepted, it will be because they are easy for the compiler to follow and for the reader to understand, well thought-out and attractive (which indeed most of them generally are), and not because they are 'right' historically. In point of fact, the ascendancy and survival of bibliographical practices has probably depended more on brutal and ignorant power politics than on any benign or objective process of logical succession. Such being the likelihood, the encouragement of dissenting practices is perhaps worthy in its own right.

Addressing 'the whole educated community' thus becomes less than a useful guideline, all the more so considering the proliferation and increasing sophistication of our various specialized learned communities. Adopting bibliographical practices that reflect the ideals of uniformity too easily leads to bureaucratic insensitivity; and adapting bibliographical practices to special circumstances too easily results in an eccentricity that subverts the compiler's cause. Whether guided by necessity or convenience, by recourse to intelligence and sensitivity or simply by feelings of yin and yang, the compiler steers a course between the two worthy ideals of bibliography.

DELIMITATIONS OF SCOPE

Wilson has proposed five specifications for bibliographical instruments,[6] which will underlie much of this text. The first, called 'domain'—'the set of items from which the contents of the work, the items actually listed, are selected and drawn'—will be discussed in Chapter VI, since it is concerned essentially with source work. The second specification is the heart of this chapter: 'the principle or principles according to which items represented . . . have been drawn from the domain'.

A bibliography on a chosen topic should be complete and comprehensive within limitations that need to be understood by the compiler and readers alike. Omissions are inexcusable. A few of the exclusions may be outrageous, bizarre, impossible to imagine, except in the unpredicted existence of materials (writings in Chinese characters, accounts printed many years ago in obscure weekly newspapers, or jig-saw puzzles); their omission can be implicit. At the other end of the spectrum are plausible materials that, for any number of reasons, have been consciously excluded. The more controversial the decision on exclusion, the more it needs to be announced and explained in detail in the introduction. Between the two extremes will lie some indifferent decisions: unannounced they could mislead some readers while announcing them could strike others as pedantic. Often the announcement can be woven into statements describing the material in question, especially since such statements are likely to enliven the message of the introduction.

The criteria for inclusion or exclusion, the 'selection principles' involved, are the means by which the scope of a bibliography comes to be shaped. Through them, the topic comes to achieve its unity. Those who like to work systematically in matters of scope and organization may find it useful to recall the five universals of human knowledge, as formulated by 'classificationists'— personality, matter, energy, space and time; and next to work out what these abstractions can mean and how their insights might be usefully applied.

Any item appropriate to a list will by its nature have two Platonic realities. It occupies space, and will continue to do so through foreseeable time, thus assuming a physical form. It also consists of content—that is, a message, verbal, intellectual, artistic, or spiritual (however such terms may be defined), sent by an original creator, modified by intermediary producers, and eventually perceived by an audience of readers. In many decisions on scope, the compiler will find it convenient to ask which of the two is primarily under consideration, although both are elements of any object that might be appropriately cited in a bibliographical list. The title, for instance, describes the content and at the same time names the physical object; the imprint, by identifying the producer of the physical object, also tells where both the content and the physical object can, or at one time could, be obtained.[7]

Physical Form

In matters of scope, there are five considerations associated with the physical form.

1. Medium.   The term 'bibliography' implies books, which can be defined narrowly as the hard-cover products of trade publishers, or broadly in terms of the so-called generic book. The latter includes not only trade and other books but also printed matter of all kinds: pamphlets, anthologies, government publications, dissertations, reports, conference proceedings and a wide range of continuations, from scholarly journals to popular magazines, annual reports, newsletters, newspapers, serials, announcements and the like.

From books it is a short step to such other printed documents as maps and music; then on to manuscripts and other unpublished materials—letters, personal records and texts in the hand of the creator or as copied by another hand; on to audio-visual documents—sound recordings, slides, motion pictures and video tapes and multi-media creations; and on to computer programs and such data archives as can hold still long enough to be described. Most of the various 'non-books' are twentieth-century innovations and consequently have been less frequently cited in our bibliographical records, with the result that they usually fit into mixed lists with some awkwardness. The compiler often finds it appropriate to exclude all materials of a particular medium — preferably on the basis of their relevance to the literature being covered and the reader's need for them, sometimes excusably on grounds of accessibility; but hardly of course because of the cumbersomeness of citation.

2. Bibliographic Level.   The materials further need to be viewed in terms of a fairly new concept among bibliographers, called *level*. Wilson's third specification, for instance, poses the question of 'how it is determined what is to count as a unit for listing and description.' Thinking in relative terms produces three levels. The basic and middle one is *monographic*, for self-contained works. Below is the *analytical* level, concerned with parts of works: an article in a periodical, an essay in an anthology, a journal review, a newspaper notice, a map or picture from an atlas or album, or even an internal passage from a text. Above is the *collective* level, which names the journal or newspaper, anthology, atlas or assemblage.

Only recently has the word 'level' come to be used, although the concept has long been around as reflected, for instance, in the classic differences in our practices for citing books as distinct from periodical articles. Precision in applying the concept of a collective level may prove useful in damning and deterring those tempted to formulate such maddening and intimidating citations as 'Marx, Karl. *Complete Works*', with no further particulars. Admittedly it may prove necessary to define exactly what a collection may or may not comprise, i.e., a common title, a numbering scheme for the parts; but also perhaps provenance, subject matter, or physical location. Apart from an original publisher, who may or may not be recognized for the collecting? As for the analytical level, what depth of detail might be identified beyond that of periodical articles, chapters of books, entries in reference sources, or bands on a sound recording? When only one paragraph on page 573 addresses our topic, can we cite that paragraph only, or must we settle for the whole book? The absence of any formal name to cite, and the prospect of specifying precise passages in the annotation, has probably deterred many a compiler from allowing the bibliography to degenerate into a presentation of miscellaneous evidence addressing the topic. For all their devoted efforts, of course, library cataloguers have never been all that successful in knowing when to settle for a single entry for a whole set, or which level to choose for a main entry. Compilers enjoy the advantages of perspective and of a finite universe, but still need to consider the options.

The compiler may conveniently and justifiably decide to exclude certain levels, on grounds that they are not appropriate for his readers and to his literatures; or he may accommodate two, or all three, through separate citations or cross-references. The list may thus include books only, or books and articles but not complete journals, or journal titles only but none of the individual articles in them, or both the collective units and their parts. Similarly, citations of other media may describe atlases and/or single maps, record albums and/or particular selections, whole archival record groups or collections and/or specific letters and documents.

3. *Circumstances of Production.* In fixing the scope of the list, it may be appropriate to consider the production of the items in question. Items may be in or out on the basis of *time*—when they were produced (for instance, excluding all items before 1550 or 1900, or after 1945); or *place*—where they were produced (including British or American imprints only); or the *conditions* under which they were produced (excluding, or perhaps relegating to annotations or an appendix, those items that were prepared from other than authentic forms of the text). The term 'production' may apply either to the printing, publication or later emendation of the physical form; and for audio-visual materials, this production could involve either the site of the performance or the location of the party responsible for the 'release'.

A chronological delimitation is often basic to the very purpose of the list—for instance, lists of early imprints of editions published during a writer's lifetime. In other lists, it is understood that entries will run up to the current moment, or as close to it as possible. A terminal date can be annoying, since major writings always have the habit of turning up just after the door has been shut. The date can be deceiving as well, since publication dates are often fixed by circumstances other than the event of making copies available to the public.[8] Even so, the compiler must reconcile himself to a terminal date, and announce it in the introduction.

4. *Features of the Physical Object.* Many lists exclude items with fewer than sixteen, fifty or ninety-six pages, mostly by way of distinguishing 'books' from 'ephemera'. Speciality lists may also be devoted to books printed on vellum or bound in alligator skin; to miniature or oversized books; to those illustrated by Rubens or Picasso, or containing added pictures of lions, or maps of Tennessee, or dedicatory songs; or to items from the library of Mathias Corvinus, Matthew Arnold or some other person. (Such considerations tend to overlap with the intellectual subjects, discussed in '6' below.)

5. *Endorsement of Location.*   Compilers today are expected to have
laid hands on, carefully examined and specifically proofread the
information in all particulars for the items they list. Their citations
are expected to be usable in the operation known to librarians,
bibliographers and subject specialists alike as 'verification'. Prior to
the nineteenth century, bibliographers commonly copied information from their predecessors without even necessarily providing
an acknowledgement. The result was a succession of perpetuated
errors, bibliographical 'ghosts' (works announced or listed but
presumably never issued), and a wide range of problems to vex,
challenge, and sometimes to exalt today's bibliographical specialists. Since the rise of modern academic scholarship, the compiler
is now required to attest to the existence of all the items cited. The
bibliographer may be allowed in very special circumstances and
for valid reasons best made explicit, clearly to signal an entry as not
examined. Fortunately, thanks to library loan practices, there is a
decreasing need for such expedients. In the case of audio-visual
materials, the attestation may involve either the existence of a
physical item purported to contain a given text, or the actual
presence of that text as promised; and the compiler who has
actually seen or heard the presentation will probably want to
mention the fact. It is understood that to cite is to sanction: the
compiler attests to authoritative documentation.

Under the circumstances, bibliographical compilation and
library collection development have often enjoyed a mutually
beneficial relationship. The emerging bibliography becomes the
order or desiderata list for the library's acquisitions programme,
which then turns up copies for its own collections that the compiler
can examine. Traditionally, lists of titles limited to the holdings of
particular collections have been defined as catalogues and not as
bibliographies. Exceptions could perhaps be allowed when the
libraries in question (personal or institutional) could claim an
unassailable mastery of the resources in the designated subject area,
so that the catalogue is tantamount to a comprehensive bibliography. With the advent of rapid and extensive photocopying —
and to the extent that we can ever circumvent that descriptive
bibliographical work which requires the physical item to be
described with a precision of detail for which photocopy evidence

is not trustworthy—the classic distinction between catalogues and enumerative bibliographies may tend increasingly to be confused. It is again a case of the scruples of modern scholarship having placed demands on libraries that produce great collections, great co-operative programmes, and great bibliographic projects.

But how much can photocopies of any kind—microfilms, xerox and other prints, even facsimiles—be trusted? The answer is that we do not know and cannot tell. Using the Platonic distinction, the photocopy as a physical form is comparable to a translation of the intellectual content. It is a copy, convenient in its own right, but not the same as the original. Just as the translator may fail us, quite innocently, and introduce a misleading concept, so the photocopy may conceal or bring out a misleading visual image. Analytical bibliographers have made much of the conceal-ment in photocopies of cancelled title pages—facts that are readily apparent when one examines the original, and that indicate different circumstances of production of the physical book.[9] On a microfilm, the photographer's omission of a particular opening of the book can go undetected. Manuscript annotations may be distorted. The problem, once again, is that we can not tell what our eyes fail to observe. Under the circumstances, the more scrupulous the compiler, and the more critical the relationship he wishes to establish between the literature and its readers, the more he will feel impelled to mention the fact that he has worked with photocopies.

Intellectual and Artistic Content

There are five criteria concerning intellectual and artistic content as related to the 'text' or 'work' as distinguished from the 'book'.

6. *Subject Matter.*   The unifying factor in many bibliographical lists may not involve subjects at all: the factor may be all of the writings by an author or group of them, for instance, or imprints of a locality, or works in a given medium. The most common lists, however, are those devoted to writings on particular subjects. For such lists, or when the definition is a mixture of restricting factors (early Idaho art books, or Icelandic recordings of Italian opera, or writings by philosophers on gardening), special efforts will be

needed to keep the subject in its proper focus. One obvious word of warning involves a watchful eye for the vagaries of terminology. Terms migrate, meaning different things to different authors at different times; and this may become apparent only as the work progresses.

At the very outset the compiler must consider in a general way the relevance of the texts involved to the subject under consideration. Relevance is the operative concept; and it varies in kind and in degrees. For instance, a bibliography of Albert Schweitzer might cover books and articles devoted exclusively to Schweitzer, most of which will have Schweitzer's name in their titles. It might also include rather general works on theology, Africa, organ music or medical missionaries, not to mention anthologies of the lives of great men, few if any of which will name Schweitzer in their titles. There are also writings on totally different subjects in which Schweitzer is quoted as an example, as well as the miscellaneous contemporary documents that mention Schweitzer. As the scope includes more of the latter materials, the size of the bibliography grows. The usefulness is almost certain to increase, along with the 'static'. Above all, the effort required of the compiler is multiplied many times over. Books devoted exclusively to a subject can usually be copied from subject headings in library catalogues; writings with casual mention of the subject require an extensive search and usually luck as well, but are what can make a list particularly valuable. The concept of relevance is a matter to which information scientists have devoted extensive research and produced significant refinements that may need to be investigated as the limited needs of the compiler come to be extended. [10]

The general rule is to err always on the side of inclusion. This practice can get out of control, for instance, so as to admit articles in general encyclopaedias, passing mention in standard histories and reference books, even entries in dictionaries. Alarmed by such prospects, the compiler may be tempted to re-examine the topic itself, and to look for a narrower definition of it; but with the needs of the intended readers taken into account, this narrowing of definition is likely not to be what is called for. It may be more appropriate to resort to criteria of quality or related factors (see '10' below). On the other hand, calling attention to the obscure, offbeat, distant or unsuspected is exactly what makes many a bibliography invaluable. Just as cataloguers have been discovering that the subject control over library collections is far and away the most problematical aspect of their responsibility, so compilers will both fear and look forward to wrestling with the subject matter of their topics, at the policy level and for as many particulars as possible.

7. *Circumstances of Creation.*   The creator or creators of the text, or the text itself, like the producer or producers of the book, may be identified or excluded on grounds that are chronological (authors born before 1800 or deceased after 1750, or texts written after 1865), or geographical (authors born in Quebec, or who lived in Paris in the 1920s, or texts written in Guadalajara). Time and place are absolutely basic, and also subject to differing interpretations depending on the circumstances of the project, whether in matters of the physical (*see* '3' above) or the intellectual book.

8. *Language or Languages.*   The works cited may be in English or other specified languages, in Western alphabets, with all languages transliterated or only in the language of original creation. Those compilers who wish to exhibit their knowledge of Albanian should be advised to consider how many of their readers might find such writings useful;[11] on the other hand, the compiler's annotation—based on his considered appraisal of the text itself— might indeed be of special interest.

9. *Objective.*   Like St Augustine's sermons, writings will educate, entertain, and exhort; and most of them do one of these better, or at least more obviously, than the other two. In the interests of helping the reader, it is often appropriate to exclude the ponderous dissertations, the imaginative belles lettres or the polemical documents relating to a subject; and surprisingly it is possible to do just this, so long as the compiler remembers to err on the side of inclusiveness.

10. Endorsement of Quality.   A very important controversy rages between honourable opponents: Must all bibliographies be complete, or is there not an even greater need for selectivity? Reasonable readers will protest the need to argue at all. There are two kinds of lists—those that make recommendations to the reader and those that establish the historical record. Why pit the two against each other? The compiler will inevitably find himself ambivalent.

Out of a spirit that mixes service and superiority, the compiler sees his duty, as Lawrence Wroth has put it, 'to display the significance of his wares.'[12] The compiler's highest responsibility to his readers and to his literature, the noblest use of his faculties and his worthy duty to scholarship, is to promote the excellent, recognizing in passing the pedestrian and damning or suppressing the false and incompetent. A bibliography, if it deserves critical approbation, must itself reflect the critical process: fools and cowards are part of the problem, not the solution.[13]

It is also the compiler's duty to concentrate his labours on the task of uncovering and presenting the literature, and to honour the readers' right to pass their own judgement. Besides, as Stokes observes, by ignoring some writings in deference to only the 'best books', the compiler undermines his work as an authoritative specialist, leaving readers to ponder whether the omissions reflect on his good taste or incompetence.[14] The difference between considered value judgement, outright prejudice and the seat of the compiler's pants is often not easy to distinguish. 'Bibliography is only useful,' according to Renan, 'when it is complete.'[15]

The weight of the argument—and there is a lot of weight on both sides—slightly favours the side of comprehensiveness, especially since the compiler has several hidden weapons at his disposal. In many instances annotations will pass judgement of their own accord, whether in matters of triviality, incompetence or redundancy. Inferior titles may be relegated to an unannotated appendix, or mentioned in passing in the annotations for the major works. However conspicuously cruel, such egalitarianism can be less mischievous than one might fear.

In the cause of intellectual quality, it is occasionally possible for the compiler to hide behind criteria of physical form (*see* '1' to '5' above). For instance, texts with fewer than 1,000 or 5,000 words may be excluded, thus eliminating the recognized authority's condensation of his truths in an after-dinner speech, publication of which justified his honorarium; or alternatively, such lesser efforts can be cited in passing in the course of an annotation, along with the various translations into Burmese and Serbian. The danger is that such objective criteria would also eliminate valuable writings as well, perhaps the terse critical review of the text, crammed with perspectives, insights, reservations and new facts.

In a selective (or as sometimes called, 'critical') bibliography, the primary function of the work is consciously focussed: now instead of endorsing, defining and promoting a topic in general, the compiler endorses, defines and promotes particular component parts of and attitudes toward the topic, for whatever reasons.

The Physical and Intellectual Book

The last of our criteria of scope involves considerations that concern both the physical and intellectual book.

11. Best Evidence.   When a work is cited, it should be cited either in all presentations, or in only the most authoritative and canonical presentation. The compiler in effect endorses not only the copy he has seen, but implicitly the copy he wants others to see. The prevalent distinction may hold that catalogues list specific copies while bibliographies list titles in general; but this merely begs a further question: how much should the compiler be concerned with what descriptive bibliographers call the 'ideal copy'?[16]

The vast majority of texts now are printed and published only once, and for these there is no problem. For particularly important or monumental writings, especially works of literature, the compiler will often need to do some further work. Sometimes there will be a good deal of work, and often the final answer will remain problematical. Should the London or New York edition be cited, or both, and if so, together or separately? Is the second edition preferable to the first, or merely a new printing from old plates, or a new setting of type, with old errors corrected and new errors added? The key is in knowing how and when to be suspicious; obviously a compiler needs to be versed in book production practices in general (bibliography in the historical and analytical sense), and the publishing history of the author and the field in particular. When books or monographic publications are concerned, a check against many standard general and subject bibliographies will call attention to different options. Sometimes two copies must be compared side-by-side in search of variant statements. Words like *revised and enlarged edition* often suggest the preferable of two copies, and the total number of pages will indicate the existence of different settings of type. Even articles, especially by scrupulous authors, can be reprinted in corrected or updated versions, often in obscure journals or anthologies for the specialist. Obviously, the closer the compiler works with and as part of the scholarly community concerned with the literature, the better. In such activities, the work of the compiler benefits from a background in analytical and textual bibliography; and one must protest the principle behind D. F. McKenzie's suggestion that 'it would be preposterous now to demand of [some bibliographies] any great sophistication' in matters involving the textual transmission processes. [17]

There are two slightly different questions involved in citations for works that exist in several different forms. How much homework needs to be done by the compiler; and how much of the findings need to be stated for the reader? For some readers, the fuller the amplification of detail, even ostensibly tedious ones, the more useful the list will be. In other instances, the reader may need only to be alerted to possible problems. The compiler must decide how much the reader needs and wants to be bothered. [18]

Conventional wisdom sometimes proposes the distinction between descriptive and systematic bibliography to be one of ends: the former treats physical objects, the latter intellectual content. Such a distinction is of course mischievous to both inquiries. Much as a whole generation of descriptive bibliographers has been trying to shake off W. W. Greg's definition of his work as 'the study of books as physical objects irrespective of their contents', [19] so those scholars who make and use bibliographical lists sad to relate will probably some day need to re-evaluate many of their bibliographical records if they are to be scrupulously concerned with what is known as 'best evidence'.

Another distinction between the two inquiries, less conspicuous but very important and ultimately worrisome, involves means. The descriptive bibliographer conceives of an ideal citation, the best possible substitute for the book itself formulated in terms of the production of the physical book. From this he works down, compromising along 'degressive' lines as may be appropriate and necessary. In contrast, the compiler starts with the briefest sufficiency of a citation, compromising by way of expanding the statement as may be necessary and appropriate. Both are fairly secure in matters of theory and those involving physical form, but in matters of practice and those involving intellectual content each runs some risk of inadequacy to the appropriate end. The luxury of the citations of 'descriptive bibliographers' can too easily focus attention on distinctions that will almost certainly not affect the sense of the content at all; while the meagreness of the citations of 'systematic bibliographers' can too easily result in the concealment of important differences in content that the reader should know about.

PERIPHERIES

The compiler needs to be forewarned that there are surprises in scope that will emerge in the course of research, usually having to do with peripheral areas. As the compiler's work progresses, he may discover that his strict delimitations ultimately distort the integrity of the topic as he intended it, or make for difficulties that are really not worth the effort. A Spanish project may make better sense if Portugal is included; or an Iberian project may prove to be just as useful and much easier with Portugal excluded. A study of fish ought, or ought not, to include whales and other aquatic mammals. The problem becomes one not only of deciding what to include but also of planning a search for this material. Such matters are rarely irrational, although they may strike the compiler this way; they are merely unpredictable.

It is sound advice to begin with the scope defined as narrowly as possible. Do not be carried away by love for, fascination with or belief in the importance of the subject. Admittedly the road is unknown: might it not in fact be easier, and more enlightening, to select the largest appropriate topic and then to delimit with the advantage of perspective? But the opposite can also be true: a narrow marked trail can often be expanded into a broad highway without too much loss of efficiency, while the vast perspective can be discouragingly unhelpful, both poignant and confusing. The advice is sound, although probably less than a majority of the world's productive compilers can honestly claim to have heeded it from the outset of their labours.

NOTES

1. Robert M. Schmitz, *Preparing the Research Paper* (New York: Holt, Rinehart & Winston, 1957), pp. 7–8.
2. Bourton, 'Subject Bibliographies' (1959), p. 7.
3. Walter J. Ong, 'The Writer's Audience is always a Fiction', *PMLA*, 90 (1975), 9–21, may not be as immediately relevant to the topic as its title would suggest, but predictably it is worth reading.
4. Jacques Barzun and Henry F. Graff, *The Modern Researcher* (3rd ed., New York: Harcourt Brace Jovanovich, 1977), p. 27.
5. Batts (1978), in the example shown on pp. 170–1, suggests many of the dimensions to this problem.
6. Wilson. *Two Kinds of Power* (1968), pp. 59–62. Bates, 'Rigorous Systematic Bibliography' (1956) implies the importance of Wilson's construction.
7. The watershed study of this distinction, surveying earlier developments and leading to most of the later discussions, is Eva Verona, 'Literary Unit versus Bibliographical Unit', *Libri*, 9 (1959), 79–104. Among the important later discussions, see G. Thomas Tanselle, 'Bibliographers and the Library', *Library Trends*, 25 (1977), 745–62.
8. Various dimensions to the matter are thoughtfully explored in Robert N. Broadus, 'The Problem of Dates in Bibliographic Citations', *College and Research Libraries*, 29 (1968), 387–92.
9. The literature on the subject is not as large or as specific as it

needs to be. Among the writings, *see* William A. Jackson, 'Some Limitations of Microfilm', *Papers of the Bibliographical Society of America*, 35 (1941), 281–8; Laurence A. Cummings, 'Pitfalls of Photocopy Research', *Bulletin of the New York Public Library*, 65 (1961), 97–101; Franklin B. Williams, Jr, 'Photo-Facsimiles of *STC* Books: A Cautionary Check List', *Studies in Bibliography*, 21 (1968), 109–19; and S. W. Reid, 'Definitive Editions and Photocomposition', *Papers of the Bibliographical Society of America*, 72 (1978), 321–6. The vital question of what exactly the compiler saw and examined is well illustrated in the brief note by A. C. Zachlin, 'On Literature Citation', *Science*, 107 (1948), 292–3.

10. Among the writings on the concept of relevance, *see* Wilson, *Two Kinds of Power* (1968), *passim*; also, as an introduction to the conceptions of information science, Tefko Saracevic, 'Relevance: A Review of and a Framework for the Thinking on the Notion in Information Science', *Journal of the American Society for Information Science*, 26 (1975), 321–43. Typically the notion is applied more to matters of subject indexing than definition of scope; *see* W. J. Hutchins, 'The Concept of "Aboutness" in Subject Indexing', *ASLIB Proceedings*, 30 (1978), 172–81.

11. The point is well illustrated by the frequent appearance in the catalogues of libraries with major music collections (including, alas, ones I myself have been associated with) of an 1835 book by a celebrated music lexicographer, one Pietro Lichtenthal, entitled, *I capelli considerati sotto verj aspetti e mezzi per conservarli*.

12. Quoted in Fredson Bowers, *Principles of Bibliographical Description* (Princeton: Princeton University Press, 1949), p. 34.

13. Among the landmark essays are L. Stanley Jast, 'Bibliography and the Deluge: I Accuse', *Library Association Record*, 38 (1936), 353–60; and Stanley Pargellis, 'Gesner, Petzholdt, *et al*', *Papers of the Bibliographical Society of America*, 53 (1959), 15–20; also his 'Some Remarks on Bibliography', *College and Research Libraries*, 7 (1946), 206–9. Related to this discussion in its basic arguments is the question of selectivity and comprehensiveness in library collection programmes, as discussed in Margit Kraft, 'An Argument for Selectivity in the Acquisition of Materials for Research Libraries', *Library Quarterly*, 37 (1967), 284–95, with an important response by Hans Lenneberg, 38 (1968), 286–90.

14. Best developed in his *Bibliographical Control and Service* (1968), p. 60, worth consulting particularly in so far as my argument could conceivably be viewed as a distortion of his basic point.

15. Quoted in Campbell, *Theory*, (1896), p. 2.

16. The concept is explained in G. Thomas Tanselle, 'The Concept of Ideal Copy', *Studies in Bibliography*, 33 (1980), 18–53. The concluding discussion is particularly appropriate to the matters treated here.

17. 'Printers of the Mind', *Studies in Bibliography*, 22 (1979), 61.

18. For further on the matters discussed here *see* Roy Stokes, 'Descriptive Bibliography: Its Definition and Function', *Papers of the Bibliographical Society of Canada*, 18 (1979), 19–25.

19. 'Bibliography: A Retrospect', in *The Bibliographical Society, 1892–1942: Studies in Retrospect* (London: The Bibliographical Society, 1945), p. 25.

CHAPTER III

Citation Style

Working out an appropriate style will often prove to be the compiler's most vexing assignment. Most of the other producers of bibliographical citations have the advantage of rigid established practices: Library cataloguers have their different codes of descriptive rules, producers of continuing series their codified procedures, even descriptive bibliographers their classic formularies. Compilers instead have only general guidelines, and contradictory ones at that. They should expect to encounter more awkward moments and tiresome decisions than they would have wished for, often for reasons having to do with the interests of tailoring their presentations to the intended readers, but often also because no one single authoritarian system has ever proven wise and aggressive enough to suppress the other aspirant systems.

A compiler working with a particular publisher may be fortunate enough to have a 'house style' dictated to him. Typically, an editor with forty years' experience and a heavy hand will cite the law and interpret it with awesome finality for the humble and terrorized compiler. Editors and compilers alike usually base their practices on the bibliographical style manuals, the most important of which as of this writing are Judith Butcher's *Copy-Editing: The Cambridge Handbook* for British practice; *The Chicago Manual of Style* for American and British practice; and the Modern Language Association's *MLA Handbook*, or the Library of Congress's *Bibliographical Procedures and Style* for American practice. In addition, an *American National Standard for Bibliographic References* has been prepared by the American National Standards Institute. (These are cited in this text, respectively, as *Butcher, Chicago, MLA, LC,* and *ANSBR*. Full references, along with a list of other major style manuals, are cited in the Supplement to this chapter.) These manuals will often disagree with each other, which will be understandable and apparent. More serious to the compiler who has decided to follow one of them, each will fail to prescribe for many of the specific decisions that will inevitably arise.

Compilers have also been encouraged to follow the practices of library cataloguers, on grounds of convenience, authority, and compatability. Cataloguing practices offer handy arbitrary solutions to citation problems; the solutions will be based on elaborately considered and carefully presented codes, involving predicaments that may scarcely have occurred to the compiler; and the final reader of a bibliography will be all the more grateful for being able to move directly from an entry in a list to the same entry in a library catalogue. The venerable distinction—a catalogue describes specific copies at hand, a bibliography lists items in general—is becoming irrelevant and obsolete, thanks to modern communications; we are really not far away from the classic vision of 'separate, uniform bibliográphic records, which can be freely interchanged and variously arranged'. [1]

Admittedly the cataloguing community has rarely agreed very well on its codes, rules and interpretations that have changed over the years and no doubt always will and should continue to evolve. The latest code—the second edition of the *Anglo-American Cataloguing Rules* [2] (hereafter abbreviated as *AACR2*), of course, is arguably the most controversial of all the codes. Furthermore, recent cataloguing philosophy has been moving away from authoritarian ideals, whether out of a concern for the needs of the readers or the labour-intensive costs entailed. How much the less authoritarian ambience of today is also thereby less authoritative for the closely examined needs of learned audiences, and how much the universal dimensions of the cataloguer's concern for readers in general can also sustain the compiler's concern for specifically defined specialist readers are matters for compilers to ponder as they ask not whether but when to follow the

cataloguers. The compiler's world, being intentionally circum-
scribed, may thus be happier for being less rule-bound. But it is all
the more incumbent on the compiler to silence an ancient legend
that defines bibliographers as merely incompetent cataloguers,
perhaps best done as compilers come to examine some of the
planning that has gone into our cataloguing codes and practices.

Whether for purposes of applying, adapting, or devising
citation style, it is important for the compiler to know what the
options are and what principles lie behind them. The decisions may
be all the more painful in that typically they are petty, as befits
cryptic statements; but the outcome can be satisfying, even if the
victory is rarely complete. The rightness of the decisions,
furthermore, will seldom be appreciated by most readers, since one
of the qualities of good style is its inconspicuousness: style becomes
convincing by appearing to be perfectly natural. The various
decisions at hand all involve the fourth of Wilson's specifications,
the 'information we can expect to find about an item, given that it
will be represented as a unit'; and these can be grouped under three
headings: *elements*, what facts need to be included in the citation?
sequence, in what order should they be arranged? and *design*, what
in the way of punctuation, typography, and layout will be useful in
order to clarify the statements?

WRITINGS ON BIBLIOGRAPHICAL STYLE. Most general writings will include
only a brief and casual discussion: for example, Higgins (1941), pp. 16–23
and 27–32; Robinson (1963), pp. 19–26 in the 1979 ed.; Olschki (1977);
Vianello (1970); and Baer (1961), pp. 13–30. Barnard (1960), while brief, is
also perceptive; Cowley (1939) chapter 10 is especially interesting for his
early discussion of 'Manuscripts and Other Awkward Material', pp.
143–77; and Picard (1974) uses the topic to investigate many interesting
peripheries. The broader perspectives of modern information science,
implied in Wilson (1968), are well developed by Richmond (1972). John
Menapace, 'Some Approaches to Annotation', *Scholarly Publishing*, 1
(1970), 194–205, is an imaginative essay that suggests some of the compiler's
options.

Style manuals are the specific concern of DeAmorim (1980), Krummel
and Howell (1979), and R. A. Sencer's brief 'A Study of Style Manuals', in
the Society of Technical Writers and Publishers, *National Convention:
Proceedings* (New York, 1957), pp. 54–7. Many of the general guides to

research, as listed in the first bibliographical note in Chapter 6, can also serve as style manuals, as can many of those cited in the notes in Chapter 7. For the most part, however, these discussions are derivative and simplified, mostly based on the style manuals themselves, if sometimes focused to reflect the special characteristics of particular scholarly communities.

The rapprochement between cataloguing practices and bibliographical citation style, implicit in much of the literature on bibliographic control, is promoted specifically in Brown's *Manual* (1906), especially pp. 45–66 ('Compiling of Bibliographies or Catalogues') and by Mangouni (1974). Williamson (1977) offers far and away the most substantial exploration of the specifics. The historical background is surveyed in Dorothy May Norris, *A History of Cataloguing and Cataloguing Methods, 1100–1850* (London: Grafton, 1939). Earlier British practices, centring around Panizzi's ninety-one rules, have been studied by Barbara McCrimmon, most recently in 'Whose Ninety-One Rules: A Revisionist View', *Journal of Library History* 18 (1983), 163–77. American events are discussed in Kathryn Luther Henderson, ' "Treated with a Degree of Uniformity and Common Sense": Descriptive Cataloging in the United States, 1876–1975', *Library Trends*, 25 (1976), 227–71. London (1980) covers much of this material as well. Paul Dunkin, *Cataloging U.S.A.* (Chicago: American Library Association, 1969) explores some of the common sense in question, while Tanselle (1977) investigates some of the major ambiguities of cataloguing practice, such as may undermine its usefulness to descriptive bibliographers.

ELEMENTS

Here are two prototypical citations, one for a book and the other for a periodical article:

Smith, Geoffrey, and Maria Martini. *Queen Christina's Library.* (Great Royal Collections, no. 8.) 2nd ed. London: Netherhall Gardens Books, 1937. 3 vols.
Brown, Nancy. 'Endo's Imagery in *Silence.*' *Modern Language*, 47 (July 1973), 143–149.

These examples include several basic kinds of statement, generally known as 'elements' (sometimes also as 'data elements' or as 'tags', notably in computer applications where they are associated with particular 'fields' of information): namely, the *author*, or authors, or other parties responsible for creating the text; the *title*, whether of the unit itself or of the larger entity of which it is a part (i.e., at the monographic, analytic or collective levels); the *imprint* (city, publisher, date; or for periodical articles, the volume, year, and pages); and, in this instance for the book, *other aspects* of the physical or intellectual item. Compilers unsure of such basics, or interested in reviewing them in the context of cataloguing practice, may wish to look into the discussions of 'reading a book technically' in cataloguing manuals. [3]

The rules for inclusion in a citation also govern the fullness of the statement. Barnard's classic maxim—'concise but sufficient'—is worth remembering; [4] and the meaning of the word 'sufficient' deserves a moment of reflection in its own right. Out of its implications come two more specific precepts: first, include what your readers will need and no more; second, include only such facts that can be cited properly and consistently. One can see the implications of each by viewing them in negative terms. For the first precept, do not put in facts that would leave your readers overwhelmed (for example, detailed bibliographical collations for a simple reading list), insulted (translations of titles for an obviously bilingual readership), bemused (full detailings of bureaucratic hierarchies within some corporate entries), or bored (listing all twenty-three cities in the imprint for a major international publisher). A well-conceived bibliographical list is an impressive achievement in its own right; there is no need to show off. The second precept is more technical: do not include facts in one entry when comparable accurate facts cannot be included in all other entries. [5]

The first precept is seldom as acceptable as it would appear, mainly because of our faith in serendipity. We have all appreciated gratuitous information, as we have so often seen subject fields come to life when curious interrelationships are brought out in small details. Nor is space likely to be a major consideration, since the bibliographical citation is of its nature a terse statement. As for the second precept, occasionally it can be defined, if not exactly deviously, at least arbitrarily, involving special practices that should be duly mentioned in the introduction. For instance, name forms can be 'established', converted to the forms cited according to cataloguing rules, or on the basis of what is seen in the *National*

Union Catalog, the British Museum *General Catalogue of Printed Books* or some other standard source.[6] Or they can be left in their original state as they appear on the title page, at the head of the article, or in some other acceptable source.[7] Prices can be cited from one standard source but omitted for items not cited in that source. There will also emerge a wide range of problems of defining consistency: prices change, for instance, or will be known only in foreign currency; the plates may be missing from some of the copies examined; or there may be doubt as to how much of the information cited on the title page actually constitutes the title.

Two natural inclinations are worth remembering. First, the variety and hence the quantity of important information will tend to diminish as the work of compilation progresses and compilers get their bearings. Many decisions on detail can be delayed to the middle stages of collecting entries, so long as compilers err on the side of including too much detail in their note-taking. Second, important facts will tend selectively to find their way from citation to annotation, where significance rather than consistency is the governing consideration. It is often a chore, for example, to mention that particular titles are parts of series, not so much because the facts are obscure but because some series are a mark of great distinction while others are mostly a convenience in production. The annotation rather than the citation can become the appropriate home for such series references worth selectively mentioning.

Another possibility, probably not often enough recognized by compilers, involves 'degressive' practices. The greater the consistency, the better the list; but sometimes the consistency will require great efforts *and* produce data that are irrelevant or ambiguous. The 'degressive principle', associated mainly with descriptive bibliography, allows for 'varying a description according to the difference of the period treated or of the importance of the work described'.[8] In enumerative bibliography it seems only fair to extend the principle to be governed not only by the importance of the work being described, but also by the importance of particular data elements and their formulation practices. It should address the questions, both of whether or not particular elements are to be stated at all, and of the detail and authority with which they are presented. For works now out-of-print, for instance, prices are irrelevant. The full name of a publisher may be crucial in certain imprint statements but not in others; dates can usefully separate the Walter Raleighs, the Oliver Wendell Holmeses, and the Engelbert Humperdincks, but for most other authors they are at best gratuitous and at worst precious. The compiler should certainly be allowed some freedom in adapting both the kinds of statements included, and the refinement and detail with which they are presented. Just as library cataloguers a generation ago largely reconciled themselves to 'no conflict' practices, so compilers should entertain the prospect of varying their citation practices—guided by their authoritative knowledge of the subject field and of the likely needs of their readers. It helps when the governing principles can be justified on grounds of their significance, whether subjective or objective; when the grounds can be described and defended in the compiler's Introduction; and when the compiler in good conscience can believe that the result is clear, clean, and appropriate.

The compiler will need to consider the following specific elements, with several of the typical questions of the appropriate 'concise but sufficient' detail.

Author

The author is the party or parties responsible for the creation of the text, however we may choose to define creation. An author statement may consist of full names, established in 'authority files' from official records or other 'definitive' sources; or last names with initials only, often to the reader's chagrin in working with Smiths and Browns; or exact transcriptions from the title page or caption title, a nuisance when inconsistencies occur. The text may be written by several persons, in which case the compiler must decide whether to name the second and later persons in regular or inverted order (regular order being easier to comprehend, inverted order being consistent with the form of the first name) and how many of the names to specify before resorting to *et al*. Generally, the more names included and indexed, the more interesting to specialized readers, who may recognize old acquaintances. When the creators are given such designations as 'compiler' or 'editor', the compiler of a bibliography must decide whether such specific relationships are all different and relevant enough to need mentioning.[9] Sometimes the text is an official document of an organization, written or edited by one person, so that the compiler must decide which of the two is really 'responsible for the creation' and deserves the entry. The awkwardness, ambiguity and impersonality of corporate names will naturally lead compilers to skip the author statement entirely, beginning directly with the title.[10] Often a compiler will favour an entry under a personal name, at least in bibliographical lists, the exception being instances where a whole series of corporate publications can be listed sequentially. The compiler must also decide whether to enter pseudonyms directly, giving the real name later, or to 'establish' the real name with reference to the pseudonym.[11] The former is more common in bibliographical lists, although there may be good reasons to prefer the latter. Obviously all of these names will need to be picked up in the index, where any inconsistencies will be disastrously apparent.

Title

The title speaks for itself as much as any of the elements. Sometimes there are two titles, as for periodicals, one identifying the name of the specific article, the other the journal in which it appears. The compiler may need to supply a title for the work if it has no real title; or the title may need to be translated, or qualified by a more specific identification (preceding the real title, for purposes of conveying the alphabetization; succeeding the real title for purposes of clarifying it).[12] Often, particularly for specialized audiences, frequently cited periodicals can become acronyms ('JASA', 'AHR', 'CRL'), not infrequently to the annoyance of readers outside the immediate community.[13] The compiler must decide whether abbreviations, if useful at all, should follow some established list, or be tailored for the special needs of the one list. Tailored lists have more than once made their creators look eccentric; but the established lists are usually far from perfect, and often need only obvious minor alterations to make them suited to specific needs.

Imprint

The imprint statement identifies the source responsible for the physical document. In modern books, the typical practice is to identify not the printer but the publisher, who has assumed responsibility for the intellectual content of the document as well as the physical production, marketing and distribution. Abbreviating the imprint may be appropriate for long lists of publishers' offices in many cities, or of the agents and consignees. For other nuances of practice (for instance, in citing imprint phrases like 'Published by' or 'and Co.' or 'Ltd', and in using dates not on the title page), the compiler will often settle for the practices of library cataloguers, or of the compilers of other reputable bibliographies.[14] The practice of providing only a city and a date without a publisher's name, accepted by some scholars and scholarly presses, deserves the harshest censure, since readers will gather important impressions from this information: a publisher proud enough to be named in the book itself should be proud enough to be cited by compilers. The date in all events is clearly needed, not only as a reflection of the currency of the thought but also as a reflection on the availability of the item.[15]

In periodical citations the imprint is typically understood to identify the volume and page numbers; the number of the specific issue or part when the pages do not run consecutively through a volume but are re-numbered for each issue or part; and the date that either complements or takes precedence over the volume and issue numbers. In multi-volume works, the imprint statement may apply either to the entire set—in which case it typically precedes the volume number—or only to the volume being cited, other volumes having appeared in earlier or later years or the publisher having changed in mid-stream, in which case the volume number ought to precede the imprint statement.[16]

Other information

It will usually be important to note that the work cited is other than the first edition (and if so, the compiler must decide whether such publisher's assurances as 'thoroughly revised' or 'completely re-written' really mean that); that the work is part of a series, whether numbered or unnumbered; that the text has been translated, revised, edited, or otherwise re-worked by another person whose efforts are acknowledged in the text itself; or that it is available (and likely to continue to be available) at a specified price. It may be useful to mention the exact number of pages—and notating this information can be a particular problem, complicated both by the practices of publishers and printers, and by the multiplicity of practices developed by cataloguers and bibliographers. When the physical item is important for the reader to know about, some brief mention of size,[17] or detailed collation of the gatherings[18] will be called for. The presence of special features (illustrations, maps, charts, bibliographical references, supplementary notes, an abstract in German, or the like); identification of particular copies (perhaps with their shelf marks and call numbers), whether the ones seen by the compiler, or a complete inventory, or a strategic selection; references to citations in other lists and similar 'concordances'[19]— such are among the elements that may or may not need to be included in the citation.

In citing other kinds of documents, still other kinds of statements are likely to be even more important. For maps, the area covered, however this can be formulated, should be specified. Recordings will require the names of the performers. Manuscript letters should name the addressee, as well as the repository of the original. For government documents it will be important to cite the document number, for patents the application number, for printed music the plate or publisher's number, for recordings the matrix number, for report literature the serial number from the responsible agency. For foreign-language materials, the presence of an English-language abstract is often usefully mentioned; for audio-visual materials, an accompanying guidebook may be important. How much detail is needed: i.e., for a motion picture, how many of the cast members will need to be named? For a recording of *Die Meistersinger*, are all twelve of those master singers really necessary? Such special problems all impinge on the larger question, of which data element (if any) is more important than the others so as to need to come first in the citation.[20]

Among the optional elements, the International Standard Book Number (ISBN), or its counterpart for other materials, deserves a special endorsement. An invaluable convenience in library acquisition work, it stands in time to become an essential control device for all literature, so as potentially to offer the compiler greater freedom in tailoring citation practices to particular audiences of readers. This book, as should be evident by now, intends to be suggestive rather than prescriptive; in this particular matter, the suggestion amounts to a strong recommendation.[21]

ANSBR, pp. 84–6, suggests most of the options in a convenient chart form. Just as important, the compiler should be guided by experience in the course of work with other kinds of bibliographical references and information sources: looking for entries, one looks for models. The compiler's final decisions should also be made with an eye to the annotations of the entries (as discussed in Chapter IV), since any information suitable to the one can move up or down to the other. Form rather than content becomes the governing consideration. Evaluative statements or other remarks that might seem more appropriate in the annotation, for instance, may move up into the citation when they are particularly important and can be stated consistently. When these conditions are in doubt, the annotation may be the better repository for facts that the reader ought to know about but that the compiler cannot in good conscience accommodate in the citation.

SEQUENCE

Typically the elements are presented in the order of the discussion above: author, title, imprint, other. But for special needs, other plans may be more appropriate. In captions for book reviews in most sources, both journalistic and learned, the title will come first, on grounds that the interested reader will be engaged more by the subject than by the author's name. (Appendix C of this book follows this practice.) Other arrangements, both logical and demonstrably appropriate, may be even more eccentric—for instance, the following citation in a list devoted to book illustrators:

Blake, Quentin (drawings, washes). 1971: The Birds, by
Aristophanes. English version by Dudley Fitts. 167 pp. (55
illus.) Lion and Unicorn Press (London).

Generally, the more important the element, the earlier it should
come in the citation. But one should remember that the very last
element is as conspicuous as one wishes it to be. Here, for instance,
is where prices appear in antiquarian booksellers' lists.

The 'usual' sequence is intentionally varied in the citation
practice for scientific literature involving what is still sometimes
known as the 'Harvard System'.[22] This sequence calls for the date
of publication to come after the author's name and before the title.
The reasoning is sound: all of an author's writings come to be
arranged chronologically under his name. The Harvard System is
most often used in lists that are adjuncts to scientific texts, in which
footnotes could be replaced by internal references (for example,
'Jones, 1938, p. 19', typically in parentheses). The fact that in the
bibliographical list the conventional grouping of elements is
disturbed—one part of the imprint being dislocated from the other
parts—is less important than the filing sequence; and indeed the
date can arguably be viewed as part of the statement of the author,
whose thinking in 1980 should be different from what it was in
1965.

The compiler should remember that filing sequences can be
either literal or internal. A literal filing sequence is determined by
the first difference in statement. When 'a' comes in one entry and
'b' in another, 'a' comes first; when after identical entries two
citations are identical up to the mention of a date, the earlier date
comes first. Literal filing sequence is typical of library card
catalogues and essential in computer filing systems. Either of them
can accommodate deviations, but it is really much easier if the filers
and readers in the first instance, and the computer in the second,
understand this simplest of arrangements. In contrast, the compiler
of bibliographies works with a list that will be in its final form at
one and only one time; and he enjoys the added advantage that the
printed page can be scanned quickly. For instance, works in a
designated part of the list or in the whole list can be arranged by the
date that appears at the end of the imprint statement. Editions of

the complete or collected works can appear before those for individual works; or books first, then articles and essays, then reviews, then writings about the author. Or works that refer to one kind of object (for instance, the name of a city) can be listed according to those topics as named in the titles, where the names are often in bold face type, capitals, underlined, or otherwise highlighted. Even the most literal-minded reader can be depended upon to pick up this fact after a moment or two, perhaps with a mild curse for the inconvenience, soon followed by a mild and continuing admiration for the compiler's decision to favour a more intelligent arrangement. A special arrangement of entries can be accomplished through internal filing elements, which the reader can comprehend by scanning. There is no need for a statement after the section heading, although a very brief one will be appreciated. A statement when the special arrangement ceases to be operative is more important.

DESIGN

The different elements will need to be made to stand out, through the use of punctuation and typography. It is useful to distinguish punctuation of interruption (periods, colons, commas) from punctuation of enclosure (parentheses, brackets, quotation marks, and occasionally dashes, each of which typically goes in pairs) and from typographic devices (italics, bold face, all capitals), each of which in different ways helps make some statements stand out. In all such matters, the guidelines are convention, clarity, and consistency. [23]

Different signs of punctuation, first of all, have conventional functions. A period marks a full stop, a completion of a sequence of ideas. A comma marks a breathing point. A succession of commas in a citation would thus appear to convey more of a sense of flow, more graciousness, hence more respect for the reader. In contrast, a succession of periods would convey a sense of discrete units, more logic, and hence more respect for the materials being cited. For some reason, the shorter the citation, the more periods look right. The semicolon, a relatively striking and unattractive sign, serves as a down-graded period or more often as an upgraded comma, for instance in separating the parts of a complicated imprint (an example, Cambridge, Mass.: Brown, Smith, and Co.; Columbus, Ohio: Western, Regional, and Local Press, Inc., 1932).

The colon does not really fit in the period/semicolon/comma hierarchy at all. Rather it has, in Fowler's happy expression, the special function of 'delivering the goods that have been invoiced in the preceding words'. Such is the spirit behind the felicitous use of colons as the punctuation between titles and subtitles. On the other hand, their use to separate city and publisher in an imprint, or volume and pages in a serial entry (for instance, 4: 63–5), is not entirely conventional. Similarly, it is hard to justify in citations the use of quotation marks, usually reserved for colloquialism and other statement as actually spoken, or italics, conventionally applied to foreign terms or words of emphasis. The use of such punctuation practices has to be justified not on grounds of convention but of clarity.

Clarity is mostly a matter of separating the elements so as to convey their identity, in some instances to convey the logical relationship between adjacent elements. Each of the elements may seem distinctive enough, but the possibilities for ambiguity are amply present, as the following mischievous concoction of a citation will demonstrate:

Smith, John, Wallace, Murphy, Hieronymus, Fritz, Rufus, Linus Alpheus, Habeas Corpus in the Federalist Papers, Constitution and Bill of Rights, Bulletin of the Georgia Law Club, series 3, 4, 6, 1945–57, 1893–1909.

Obviously commas cannot do the whole job: in time one can figure out that there are four authors. But we never know whether 'Constitution and Bill of Rights' is part of the title or the name of the Law Club's bulletin; or which of those numbers indicate volumes and issues, which are dates and which page numbers. Help from the compiler is most useful not only in clarifying elements but in making them stand out in their own right. Readers do browse through bibliographies in search of familiar names; they look for dates in order to get some sense of the span of coverage, or to spot the earliest or latest essays, or those written just after World War II; they hunt out the discursive treatments of their topic for their own edification, or pithy ones to assign to their less than diligent student; they recognize the endorsement of respected series, imprints, and institutions. Whatever the compiler can do to help the cause will be most appreciated.

It has also been conventional for unpublished titles (dissertations, reports, and the like) to be cited in quotation marks rather than underlined. Thanks to library co-operation and modern photographic technology, almost all titles are, by being available, in a sense published; perhaps it is now time for this distinction to be erased. Such changes can best come about as the changing tastes and attitudes of compilers reflect changing circumstances; this point again underlines the proposal that compilers should be encouraged to think in terms of underlying considerations rather than of prescribed practices.

It is for purposes of contrast that analytic-level titles are usually in quotes and monographic-level ones in italics. Just as we conventionally distinguish quoted titles of songs and short lyric poems from italicized titles of operas and long epic poems, so we distinguish titles of articles from the titles of the journals in which they are contained. In dealing with internal citations within titles (as in the Nancy Brown example cited at the beginning of this chapter), such practices are particularly helpful. This same principle probably underlies the practice of putting volume numbers in bold-face type—although somehow the effect suggests rather that the printer was using worn ink rollers. As for the hoary practice of using roman numerals for volumes in periodical citations, it must be conceded that the desired contrast is indeed achieved; but, most readers will agree, the price is too high.

The final criterion for any punctuation scheme is consistency. Consistency has to be understood partly in negative terms: any deviation from established practice is assumed to have some significance. No aspect of citation practice is so annoying, so conducive to second thoughts, to decisions as minor as they are awkward. The goal itself is understandably desirable: it reflects on the compiler's basic competence to do a job correctly, not on control of the topic, or usefulness of the research. The principle itself is also sound: do a thing in one place, do it in all comparable situations. Unfortunately, the question is one of determining what is really comparable. As a rule, for instance, we may conclude that no period is necessary at the end of a citation. But this rule is overruled by one that requires a period at the end of complete sentences, and another at the end of abbreviations. Is it not then better to reverse the first rule: periods at the end of all citations? Or is the rule simply overruled in specific instances? Not uncommonly, a compiler will find, for a given practice, twelve 'points of consistency', in three of which it works brilliantly, in six of which it is tolerable and unobtrusive, in two of which it conflicts with another practice, and in one of which it looks dreadful but for no good reason at all. In these moments the compiler will learn to appreciate the competence of a heavy-handed editor. Just as there are no atheists in the foxholes, so there are no pedants in the design and presentation of bibliographical citations.

But the job of 'styling' is not done until the last entry is typed. In the course of preparing the list, there will be dozens of small decisions, some unique, a few ostensibly unique but actually concerned with policy, just as many the other way around. In abbreviating numbers, do we use '2d' or '2nd'? With or without periods? What can we abbreviate; can we use the ampersand, do we spell out place names, or use common abbreviations, or postal abbreviations; for inclusive pages, do we repeat numbers, (1046–1047), or settle for the shortest form (1046–7), or repeat the last two digits, as is common (1046–47), or settle for a special plan such as that of the Oxford University Press, which is very sensible and legible? Can we settle for 'NY', or 'U.S.' (or 'US') or other acronyms (but 'Lpz.' for Leipzig, 'Bp.' for Budapest)? For initialed names do we use the space bar on the typewriter: is it 'C.S.' or 'C. S. Lewis'? Do we capitalize the first word of a title and all proper names; or all substantives (probably preferable in that it brings out terms for browsing, although library cataloguers have been trained to do otherwise)? As a policy decision, how much should the compiler presume to tamper with the title statement in the text itself, in the interest of the clarity and consistency of his bibliographical list?

All of these decisions ought ideally to be made in conjunction with the planning of the layout of the entries on the printed page. The graphics of bibliography, to be discussed in Chapter VII, involve considerations quite different from those treated above, and thus the two parties—the one who compiles the entries and the other who arranges them on the page—should begin talking to one another fairly early, preferably with some models at hand.

STYLE MANUALS

This discussion of the content, sequence, and punctuation of the bibliographical elements needs finally to be viewed in the light of the style manuals themselves. Below are two arrays of different citations for the same imaginary book and periodical, drawn up as best one could from the instructions in eight of the most important, and divergent, of the manuals. Obviously the differences are often insignificant; in other cases they are debatable in importance. In many cases the precise recommendation of the manual was not in evidence; and while I have called attention to the fact that MLA makes no provision for normal or inverted word order for the names of joint-authors, in numerous other instances I have importuned solutions, such as future compilers themselves will need to do. It has presumably been long understood that the manuals themselves are models more than stipulations. Thus when Chicago (12th ed., p. 374, item 16.8) can specify that 'the physical facts about a work . . . are listed on library catalog cards and on booksellers' lists but are omitted from scholarly bibliographies,' the citations devised here can protestingly reflect the policy, almost as a means of encouraging compilers to deviate, and to come up with the obvious and valid reasons for deviating. The differences between the style manuals, however prescriptive, and a standard, which *ANSBR* claims to be, is hard to comprehend. And while, in my opinion, the *ANSBR* citation ranks with LC and Harvard as the least attractive of the lot, the principles behind *ANSBR* are clearly laudable. Above all, however, it should be remembered that the purpose of this chapter is to describe principles rather than to prescribe practices.

Citation for a Book

BUTCHER[24]
Smith, Geoffrey, and Martini, Maria. *Queen Christina's Library*. Great Royal
Collections, 8. 2nd ed. London, 1937.

CHICAGO[25]
Smith, Geoffrey, and Martini, Maria. *Queen Christina's Library*. 2nd ed. Great
Royal Collections, 8. London: Netherhall Gardens Books, 1937.

MLA
Smith, Geoffrey, and [normal or inverted?]. *Queen Christina's Library*. 2nd ed.
Great Royal Collections, 8. 3 vols. London: Netherhall Gdns. Books, 1937.

HURT
Smith, Geoffrey, and Maria Martini. *Queen Christina's Library*. Great Royal
Collections, 8. 2d ed. London: Netherhall Gardens Books, 1937. 3 vols.

LC
Smith, Geoffrey, *and* Maria Martini. Queen Christina's library. 2d ed.
London, Netherhall Gardens Books, 1937. 3 v. (Great Royal Collections, 8)

ANSBR[26]
Smith, Geoffrey; Martini, Maria. Queen Christina's library. 2nd ed. London:
Netherhall Gardens Books; 1937. 3v. (Great Royal Collections, 8)

HARVARD[27]
Smith, G., and Martini, M. 1937. *Queen Christina's Library*. (Great Royal
Collections, 8.) London: Netherhall Gardens Books, 3v.

GERMAN[28]
SMITH, GEOFFREY, and MARIA MARTINI. *Queen Christina's Library*. 2. edition.
V. 1–3. London 1937 (= Great Royal Collections, 8.)

The final fillip to this discussion must remind us that the
conception of a bibliographical entry has changed frequently,
however subtly, over the course of the years. A glance at lists from
the nineteenth century and earlier will suggest a variety of different

Citation for an Article

BUTCHER[24]

Brown, Nancy. 'Endo's imagery in *Silence*', *Modern language*, 47 (July 1973), 143–9.

CHICAGO[25]

Brown, Nancy. "Endo's Imagery in 'Silence." *Modern Language* 47 (July 1973): 143–9.

MLA

Brown, Nancy. "Endo's imagery in 'Silence,'" *Modern Language*, 47 (July 1973), 143–9.

HURT

Brown, Nancy. "Endo's Imagery in Silence," *Modern Language*, XLVII (July, 1973), 143–149.

LC

Brown, Nancy. "Endo's imagery in *Silence*." Modern language, v. 47. July 1973: 143–149.

ANSBR[26]

Brown, Nancy. Endo's imagery in Silence. Modern Language. 47: 143–9. July 1973.

HARVARD[27]

Brown, N. 1973. Endo's imagery in *Silence. Modern Language*, 9: 143–9.

GERMAN[28]

BROWN, NANCY, Endo's imagery in *Silence, Modern Language*, 47 (July 1973) p. 143–9.

practices. Few of these could honestly be labelled as functionally inappropriate.[29] Today's visions of uniformity of practice in all bibliographies—truly compatible citations, rigidly controlled by standards and preferably indistinguishable from cataloguing practice, a kind of bibliographical Esperanto—are mostly twentieth-century attitudes, which may or may not still be attractive in fifty years' time.[30] More predictable if less than consoling, we should recognize that citation practices fifty years from now will almost surely be different from today's.

In some ways the design of citation styles has to be labelled as 'cosmetic'; and considering the 'labour-intensive' nature of the compiler's work and the widespread concern among scholars and publishers for 'cost-effectiveness' of every imaginable form, the tendency to view subtleties of citation design as 'mere frills' will not likely diminish. The compiler needs to develop an instinct for recognizing practices that look to be merely 'aesthetic' but that, when handled differently, might in some way affect the reader's ability to work with the list as a whole, or that, when overlooked, might lead to confusion and wrong impressions. A survey of the citation practices in the notable books listed in Appendix C will further serve to suggest how variable the practices are, and how the deviation from the norms proposed by style manuals, library cataloguers and bibliographical services—especially when interpreted by a skilled book designer—may better serve the needs of the intended readers. Considering the cost of altering the practices of our major bibliographical programmes of today, each with its millions of entries, the modest dimensions of bibliographical lists make them a particularly attractive testing ground for new citation practices.

NOTES

In the preparation of this chapter, I should like to acknowledge the special help of my colleague, Professor Kathryn Luther Henderson, in calling attention to many of the specialized writings cited here; and of my former student, John Bruce Howell, for information on the style manuals.

1. The sentiments are those of Charles Coffin Jewett (1816–68), father of America's cataloguing codes, as quoted in London (1980), p. 284.
2. London: The Library Association, 1983 (British text, With

Revisions); Chicago: American Library Association; Ottawa: Canadian Library Association, 1978 (North American text). The deliberations and controversial practices are described in *The Making of a Code: The Issues Underlying AACR2, Papers Given at the International Conference on AACR2 held March 11–14, 1979, in Tallahassee, Florida*, edited by Doris Hargrett Clark. Chicago: American Library Association, 1980. Other writings are listed in its 'Selected Bibliography', pp. 231–9. Notable among these are Phyllis A. Richmond. 'AACR2—A Review Article', *Journal of Academic Librarianship*, 6 (March 1980), 30–7; and J. A. Shinebourne, 'A Critique of AACR,' *Libri*, 29 (1979), 231–59, with further discussions, 30 (1980), 247–50. Tanselle (1977) specifically addresses the earlier version of the code ('AACR1'), although most of his criticisms apply to AACR2 as well.

3: Among the best introductions, and still to be recommended in spite of its age, is Margaret Mann, *Introduction to Cataloguing and Classification of Books* (2nd ed., Chicago: American Library Association, 1943), chapter 2 ('How to Read a Book Technically', pp. 12–29). For definitions of technical terms, the *AACR2* 'Glossary' (pp. 563–72) is valuable. Jean Peters, *The Bookman's Glossary* (6th ed., New York: R. R. Bowker, 1983) is ampler and less prescriptive. Also useful and even more extensive is Geoffrey Ashall Glaister, *Glaister's Glossary of the Book: Terms used in Papermaking, Printing, Bookbinding* (2nd ed., London: George Allen & Unwin, 1979).

4. Barnard, *Bibliographical Citation* (1960), p. 5.

5. The literature devoted to the 'concise but sufficient' concept includes, on the one side, statements mostly from scientists in search of the bibliographical quark. A good anthology of these was occasioned by G. E. McCasland, 'A Concise Form for Scientific Literature Citations', *Science*, 120 (1954), 150–2. On pp. 1038–41 the respondents—R. P. Boas, Karl F. Heumann, Charles Bishop, Eugene Garfield, and Ralph Silliman—bring out a variety of useful points, on both sides of the issue. The other side then is best reflected in the title of Phyllis A. Richmond's short article, 'Misery is a Short Footnote', *Library Resources and Technical Services*, 9 (1965), 221–4; by Thompson (1978); and by Domay (1968), whose massive study is a valuable method book for librarians as they learn

to pursue the stimulating, frustrating, and highly important task of bibliographical verification.

6. The topic of authority control is daunting even to cataloguers, whose feelings have historically blown both hot and cold under the influence of contrasting considerations. Only by establishing authoritative forms for proper names can commonalities be effectively collected. But doing so also takes much time; it tends to work against the ideal of 'natural language' access; and it ultimately calls for policy decisions in matters of conformity and tailoring, and decisions that preferably are logical, effective and consistent. Herein is suggested one of the advantages of the compiler over the cataloguer—provided of course that the compiler can make responsible, consistent, and credible decisions in the first place, once again avoiding the equation of bibliography with bad cataloguing. The compiler who wishes to study the matter can perhaps best begin with Edith K. Baecker and Dorothy C. Senghas, *A Little Brief Authority: A Manual for Establishing and Maintaining a Name Authority File* (Boston: De Doss Associates, 1978). Fuller particulars are addressed in the proceedings of the 1979 Library and Information Technology Association's institutes entitled *Authority Control: The Key to Tomorrow's Catalog*, ed. by Mary W. Ghikas (Phoenix: Oryx Press, 1982), also in the Library of Congress, *Authorities: A Marc Format* (Washington, 1981). The notion that authority work may no longer be needed has been widely suggested but, to my knowledge, never defended definitively; among the suggestions, *see* Mitch Friedman, 'A Conversation with Frederick G. Kilgour', *Technicalities*, vol. 1, no. 7 (June 1981), pp. 2–7, 19–20. Recent discussions of the topic include Jean M. Perreault, 'Authority Control, Old and New', *Libri*, 32 (1982), 124–48; Lawrence Auld, 'Authority Control: An Eighty-Year Review', *Library Resources and Technical Services*, 26 (1982), 319–30; and Kathryn Luther Henderson, 'Great Expectations: The Authority Control Connection', *Illinois Libraries*, 64 (1983), 334–6.

7. One of the valuable innovations in *AACR2* is the specification of sources of information. Rule 22.2A, for instance, lists the possible sources for the form of a name, in preferential order. Other specifications are listed in the index, p. 612, under 'Sources

of Information'. For periodical articles, it is common to take the statement in the caption title at the head of the first page of the text, for instance in preference to the statement in the Table of Contents. But discographers still argue between the statement on the record label and the one on the sleeve; and in other areas of bibliography, policies are yet to be considered. *ANSBR*, for instance, helps very little—except perhaps by calling attention to the fact that there is a problem—in proposing that 'bibliographic elements are to be recorded . . . as they appear in the original work, rather than according to special cataloging or authority rules or conventions. The exceptions to this general guideline are bibliographic elements for which national or international standards have been developed' (p. 27).

8. The literature on the 'degressive principle', more celebrated and impressionistic than extensive and systematic, apparently begins with Falconer Madan's 'memorandum' entitled 'Degressive Bibliography', *Transactions of the Bibliographical Society*, 9 (1906), 53–65, the beginning passages of which have provided the definition as quoted. The specific plan developed by Madan, E. Gordon Duff and Strickland Gibson, appears in 'Standard Descriptions for Printed Books', in the *Proceedings and Papers of the Oxford Bibliographical Society*, vol. 1 part 1 (1923), pp. 13–14, 55–64. Most of the subsequent literature—highlighted by a 1966 *Times Literary Supplement* review of William B. Todd's *Bibliography of Edmund Burke*, and subsequent correspondence—is discussed in Fredson Bowers, 'Bibliography Revisited', *The Library*, 5th series, 24 (1969), 89–128; *see also* his 'Purposes of Descriptive Bibliography, with Some Remarks on Methods', *The Library*, 5th series, 8 (1953), 1–22, especially the concluding pages. The term 'degressive' itself—in a sense the converse of 'progressive'—is commonly used in the literature of taxation, for instance to describe a rate that is constant on sums above a certain limit, but which diminished on sums counted downward below the limit. In essence it mandates practices of compromise, of working downward from the ideal and plenary citation, along systematic lines and in deference to the prospect of less rigorous bibliographical demands. It is then perhaps curious that the concept—or at least the term—should have been appropriated

mostly by descriptive bibliographers, the thrust of whose scholarship has largely invalidated the concept of plenary citations by developing new methods, studying new kinds of evidence (type, paper, now perhaps ink as well), and in general looking for ways to refine rather than compromise their statements. The relevance of the 'degressive principle' to library cataloguing seems to be suggested in the 1923 plan cited above. Cataloguers before and since, meanwhile, have followed the sense of the principle through various 'brief' and 'minimal' cataloguing programmes. Compilers have, too, of course, for instance in ANSBR's distinction between comprehensive and abbreviated citations; other specific plans need to be located and studied. The appropriateness of the concept to systematic bibliography is suggested in Madan's original 1906 essay, where for instance the 'minimum description' is viewed as appropriate 'for a mere list of works'.

9. The announced relationships between a creator, or assistant to the creator, and the text itself—whether as 'author', 'compiler', 'editor', or often involving ingenious verb forms like 'assembled by', 'authorized by', 'collected by', or 'the favorites of'—have prompted *AACR2*'s restrictive posture. The only allowable forms now are author, editor, and compiler, as specified in rule 21.1A1, and as defined in Appendix D on p. 565. See also rules 21.OD and 21.7A–C. Compilers inclined to question this practice should read Phyllis Richmond's 'AACR2: A Review Article', *Journal of Academic Librarianship*, 6 (1980), 30–7. Fuller definitions of some of the commonly used terms—which publishers may or may not choose to recognize—appear in Peters and Glaister.

10. The predilection for title entries in bibliographies is one of the interesting themes developed by Williamson (1977). The awkwardness of redundancy is well illustrated in the list of 'Major Style Manuals' at the end of this chapter: do those names really need to be cited *three* times?

11. The fullest discussion on the topic in general is still Archer Taylor and Frederic Mosher, *A Bibliographical History of Anonyma and Pseudonyma* (Chicago: Published for the Newberry Library by the University of Chicago Press, 1951). The current cataloguing picture is summarized in Bruce E. Ford, 'New Attempts to

Resolve Old Conflicts: Chapter 22 of AACR2', *Library Resources and Technical Services*, 24 (1980), 214–16. American cataloguing practice, which long provided for the establishment of the author's true name, is compromised in *AACR2* in deference to British practice, which accepts the title statement and provides for alternatives through cross references, as collected for instance in Samuel Halkett and Rev. John Laing, *A Dictionary of the Anonymous and Pseudonymous Literature of Great Britain* (Edinburgh: W. Patteson, 1882–88); new and enlarged ed. by Dr James Kennedy, W. A. Smith, and A. F. Johnson (Edinburgh, London: Oliver and Boyd, 1926–62); for the third ed. *see* John Horden, *A Dictionary of Anonymous and Pseudonymous Publications in the English Language* (Harrow: Longman, 1980). Counterpart lists for other languages are listed in Taylor and Mosher, supplemented by more recent publications as cited in the current guides to reference books like Walford, Sheehy, Arnold, and Koppitz.

12. The study of title formulations needs to be synthesized—a task greater than can be accommodated by a bibliographical note here—and pursued. It extends from the practices of conventionalization for standard works—as covered for instance in R. C. Hewett, *Anonymous Classics: A List of Uniform Headings for European Literature* (London: International Federation of Library Associations and Institutions, International Office for UBC, 1978)—to the efforts to promote precision in title statements, as advanced probably most conspicuously by Eugene Garfield and the Institute for Scientific Information in Philadelphia.

13. Standard forms for periodical title abbreviations have been proposed for sub-macrocosmic levels, but rarely adopted at the microcosmic level for reasons that are both understandable and unfortunate. 'JLH' may be the sufficient statement that identifies the *Journal of Library History* to anyone working in or near library history, but not to those working with legal handwriting, Latvian humanism, laboratory hormones, or literary hoaxes. The most extensive unified programme is the 'Coden' system developed in the United States, available on microfiche (Columbus, Ohio: American Chemical Society, 1978–), and described in A. L. Batik, 'The Coden System', *Journal of Chemical Documentation*, 13 (1973), 111–13. The British Standard Institution has its *Specification*

for the Abbreviation of Periodicals (BSS 41:48:1967); the Americ? National Standards Institute has its *Abbreviations of Titles of Periodicals* (ANSI Z39.5-1969, revised 1974); and the International Organization for Standardization has its *International Code for the Abbreviation of Titles of Periodicals* (Geneva, 1954). For an anthology of statements, *see* Leland G. Alkire, Jr, *Periodical Title Abbreviations* (3rd ed., Detroit: Gale Research Co., 1981, with annual supplements).

14. For American publishers names, suggested short forms are listed in Karen Judd, *Copyediting: A Practical Guide* (Los Altos, Cal.: William Kaufmann, 1982), pp. 168–76. As usual, the general rules for omission—the initial article, first names except with common or conflicting surnames, and corporate status designations—are sensible but not as easily applied as might be wished. Even more arbitrary are the decisions to limit the several or many city names in which a publisher has its offices, with the result that citation practices today probably err on the side on including too many of them. A prescriptive short-form policy is described in *AACR2*, section 1.4D-E. *Chicago* (13th ed., pp. 456–8) has a good, brief policy.

15. The topic is thoughtfully discussed in Robert N. Broadus, 'The Problem of Dates in Bibliographic Citations', *College and Research Libraries*, 29 (1968), 387–92.

16. This practice is illustrated in the entries for Grand (1888) and Stokes (the 1969 encyclopedia article) in the 'Bibliography' of this book, as well as in the Greg citation in note 18 below.

17. The topic has been well surveyed in B. J. McMullin, 'About the Size of It', *Journal of Library History*, 17 (1982), 429–52.

18. The standard sources for collational statement practices are W. W. Greg, 'A Formulary of Collation', *The Library*, 4th series, 14 (1934), 365–82; his *Bibliography of the English Printed Drama to the Restoration*, vol. 4 (London: The Bibliographical Society, 1959), pp. lv–lxiii; and Fredson Bowers' magisterial *Principles of Bibliographical Description* (Princeton: Princeton University Press, 1949).

19. Proposed brief statements, mostly for work with early books, are listed in Peter VanWingen and Stephen Paul Davis, *Standard Citation Forms for Published Bibliographies and Catalogs used in Rare Book Cataloging* (Washington: Library of Congress, 1982).

20. 'Non-print' materials, which long suffered for lack of any sympathy in the library and bibliographical communities, still suffer for lack of specially appropriate citation practices, although the picture is clearly improving. *ANSBR* consciously addresses the problem, as does the 13th edition of the *Chicago Manual of Style*. Within the fields themselves, the bibliographical traditions are often waiting to be developed; among the attempts at specialized bibliographical style manuals, see notes 26–9 in Krummel and Howell (1979). Nor should any author pass up the opportunity to insert a word of praise for Wilson (1955).

21. The ISBN program is described in various publishing and literary sources, notably among them K. W. Neubauer, 'The Present Status and Future Expectations of the Programme for the Assignment of International Standard Book Numbers', *IFLA Journal*, 5 (1979), 8–21. Current developments are announced in the *ISBN Review* (1977–   ), available from the International ISBN Agency, Staatsbibliothek Preussuscher Kulturbesitz, Postfach 1407, D-1000 Berlin, Germany/B.R.D.

22. The term 'Harvard system' is obscure in its origins, but has long been associated principally with the social sciences, notably anthropology, sociology, and psychology. By 1936 its practices were already being endorsed at a Royal Society conference by editors of scientific journals. While C. Langton Hewer, for one, later objected strenuously, his reservations have more to do with the appearance of the text than of the citations ('The many authors' names are interspersed in the text like the stones in a cherry pie, and produce mental indigestion unless discarded'); *see* his letter to the *British Medical Journal*, 1 (1945), 233–4. Among the more extended discussions in general, see the *Chicago Manual of Style*, i.e., pp. 384–8 in the 12th ed.; pp. 400–35 (esp. 400–5 and 420–4) in the 13th ed., where the term 'Author-Date System' is introduced.

23. This text is based largely on the article on 'Stops' in H. W. Fowler, *A Dictionary of Modern English Usage* (2nd ed. Oxford: Clarendon Press, 1965), pp. 578–92, and G. V. Carey, *Mind the Stop; A Brief Guide to Punctuation* (New ed. Cambridge: Cambridge University Press, 1960).

24. The example conforms to the bibliography example in the text (1st ed., p. 183; 2nd ed., p. 184), but deviates from the style in

the 'Selected Bibliography' (1st ed., pp. 309–10; 2nd ed., pp. 312–13). Many matters are still left for the compiler to improvise, as I have done.

25. The example is derived from the 12th edition, more prescriptive and more arbitrary for present purposes, rather than the 13th.

26. Comprehensive references, based on illustrations on pp. 38–9 for the example of a book, and on pp. 33–4 for the periodical article.

27. Adapted from the presentation in *Chicago*, 12th ed., pp. 384–8.

28. As an example of a continental citation practice of a kind, the statement would appear to be generally consistent with the provisions of Baer (1961).

29. The point is suggested and provocatively developed— admittedly with special concern for a different area of bibliography—in David F. Foxon, *Thoughts on the History and Future of Bibliographical Description* (Library Schools of the University of California, Lectures in Bibliography, 10; Berkeley, Los Angeles, 1970).

30. The recurrence of the same kinds of problems as those discussed here is suggested, for instance, in Abraham Lebowitz, 'A Common Communication Format for Machine-Readable Biblio-graphic Data', in *Toward a Common Bibliographic Exchange Format?* (Budapest: OMKDK-Technoinform; London: UNIBID, 1978), pp. 195–208.

SUPPLEMENT TO CHAPTER III

Major Style Manuals

The great number of statements, reflecting the wide range of practices, may be seen in the standard bibliographies by Mary R. Kinney, *Bibliographical Style Manuals: A Guide to their Use in Documentation and Research* (ACRL Monographs, 8; Chicago: American Library Association, 1953), and John Bruce Howell, *Style Manuals of the English-Speaking World* (Phoenix, Arizona: Oryx Press, 1983). See also the *Chicago Manual of Style*, 13th ed., pp. 685–94. The selective list below is limited to those that would appear to be particularly important, respected, widely used, and models for other manuals. It is limited to those that treat bibliographical style in more than a perfunctory manner—thus excluding, for instance, Horace Harts's venerable *Rules for Compositors and Readers* (the 'Oxford' manual), and the *Style Manual* of the U.S. Government Printing Office. Among the titles listed here, Butcher is arguably the most important British source. In addition to the American sources used in the text above (University of Chicago, the Modern Language Association, Hurt, Library of Congress, and the American National Standard), Appel and Skillin are still in wide general use. Most of the lists for scientific organizations use Harvard style. The UNISIST manual, while now dated, is still probably the best computer system for large projects, with valuable features in general. The ISBD lists probably herald many future cataloguing practices.

[American Anthropological Association]. 'Style Guide and Information for Authors', *American Anthropologist*, 79 (1977), 774–9.

American Chemical Society. *Handbook for Authors of Papers in American Chemical Society Publications.* Washington: American Chemical Society, 1978.

American Institute of Physics. *Style Manual for Guidance in the Preparation of Papers.* 3rd rev. ed. New York: American Institute of Physics, 1978.

American Medical Association, Scientific Publications Division. *Style Book: Editorial Manual.* 6th ed. Littleton, Mass.: PSG Publishing Co., 1976.

American National Standards Institute. *American National Standard for Bibliographic References.* (Z39.29-1977). New York: American National Standards Institute, 1977.

American Psychological Association. *Publications Manual.* 3rd ed. Washington: American Psychological Association, 1983.

American Society of Agronomy. *Handbook and Style Manual for ASA, CSSA, and SSSA Publications.* Madison, Wis.: American Society of Agronomy, Crop Science Society of America, Soil Science Society of America, 1976.

Appel, Livia. *Bibliographical Citation in the Social Sciences and the Humanities: A Handbook of Style for Authors, Editors, and Students.* 3rd ed. Madison, Wis.: University of Wisconsin Press, 1949. Also issued as a supplement to Gilbert J. Garraghan, *A Guide to Historical Method*, New York: Fordham University Press, 1957.

Australia, Commonwealth Government Printing Service. *Style Manual for Authors, Editors, and Printers.* Canberra: Australian Government Printing Service, 1966; 2nd ed., 1972; 3rd ed., revised by John Pitson, 1978.

British Psychological Society, Standing Committee on Publications. *Suggestions to Contributors.* Leicester: British Psychological Society, 1979.

British Standards Institution. *Bibliographical References.* (British Standard 1629:1950.) London: British Standards Institution, 1950; *Recommendations: Bibliographical References* (British Standard 1629:1976.), 1976.

Butcher, Judith. *Copy-editing: The Cambridge Handbook.* Cambridge: Cambridge University Press, 1975. 2nd ed., 1981.

Chicago Manual of Style. See University of Chicago Press.

Council of Biology Editors, Committee on Form and Style. *CBE Style Manual.* 4th ed. Washington: American Institute of Biological Sciences, 1978.

Elrington, C. R. *Handbook for Editors and Authors — The Victoria History of the Counties of England.* London: Institute of Historical Research, 1978.

Harvard Law Review. *A Uniform System of Citation.* 13th ed. Cambridge, Mass.: Harvard Law Review Association, 1982.

House Style: The Preparation and Printing of Books for Sweet & Maxwell/Stevens & Sons, W. Green & Son. London: Sweet & Maxwell, 1975.

Hurt, Peyton. *Bibliography and Footnotes: A Style Manual for Students and Writers.* 3rd ed. Berkeley: University of California Press, 1968.

International Federation of Library Associations. *ISBD: International Standard Bibliographic Description for Monographic Publications.* London: IFLA, Committee on Cataloguing, 1974. Other statements for other materials have also been issued or are in preparation.

International Organization for Standardization. *Standardization in the Domain of Documentation.* (ISO/TC 46.) The Hague: International Organization for Standardization, 1954.

Library of Congress, General Reference and Bibliography Division. *Bibliographical Procedures and Style: A Manual for Bibliographers in the Library of Congress*, ed. by Blanche P. McCrum and Helen D. Jones. Washington: Government Printing Office, 1954.

Modern Humanities Research Association. *MHRA Style Book: Notes for Authors, Editors, and Writers of Dissertations*, ed. by A. S. Maney and R. L. Smallwood. 3rd ed. London, 1981.

Modern Language Association. *The MLA Style Sheet*, compiled by William Riley Parker. New York: Modern Language Association of America, 1951; revised ed., 1954; 2nd ed., 1970. Now subsumed in the *MLA Handbook for Writers of Research Papers, Theses, and Dissertations*, ed. by Joseph Gibaldi and Walter S. Achtert, 1977.

Skillin, Marjorie E., Robert M. Gay, et al. *Words into Type*. 3rd ed., completely revised. Englewood Cliffs, N.J.: Prentice-Hall, 1974.

Tillin, Alma M., and William J. Quinly. *Standards for Cataloging Nonprint Materials: An Interpretation and Practical Application*. 4th ed. Washington: Association for Educational Communications and Technology, 1976.

Turabian, Kate L. *A Manual for Writers of Term Papers, Theses, and Dissertations*. Chicago: University of Chicago Press, 1937; 4th ed., 1973; 1st British ed., London: Heinemann, 1982. (*See* the annotation under University of Chicago Press.)

United Nations, Dag Hammarskjöld Library. *Bibliographical Style Manual*. (Bibliographical Series, 8; United Nations Document ST/LIB/ser.B/8.) New York: United Nations, 1963.

United Nations Educational, Scientific, and Cultural Organization. *UNISIST Reference Manual for Machine-Readable Bibliographic Descriptions*. (SC.74/WS120.) Paris: UNESCO, 1974.

University of Chicago Press. *A Manual of Style.* Chicago: University of Chicago Press, 1906; 11th ed., 1949; 12th ed., completely revised, 1969 (*see* esp. pp. 371–97); 13th ed., revised and expanded, now entitled *The Chicago Manual of Style*, 1982 (*see* esp. pp. 420–83). This text is not to be confused with Turabian, above, which in its early editions prescribes practices somewhat different from those in the *Manual of Style*. The differences came in time to diminish, so that the 3rd revised ed. of Turabian (1967) could claim to conform 'in general' to the 11th ed. of the *Manual of Style*.

CHAPTER IV

Annotation

FUNCTION

The compiler of bibliographies can often rely on the titles cited to convey part of the sense of the text to the reader, but rarely all of it. The author rightfully devises a title for the text that will suggest who the appropriate readers are and will attract as many readers as possible. Reviewers, librarians, compilers of bibliographies and readers may feel differently after having studied the text. Authors quickly learn, however, that fully explicit titles run to the length of titles for eighteenth-century essays and modern doctoral dissertations; even when relatively brief, they are usually deadly. Implicit titles do engage the reader, besides usually conveying some evasive but crucial aspect of the message of the text itself.

Other parts of the citation enlighten us by their implications — the author's name, the date, the reputation of the publisher, the total number of pages, the added features. But these are rarely all that is needed: citation or identification may be essential, but it is not everything. Several distinguished dissenters to the contrary,[1] there are very few bibliographies that would not benefit from annotations to their entries. One respected bibliographer has gone so far as to propose that when the content typical of annotations is sacrificed, 'drought has begun its work upon the bibliographical garden'.[2] Often the compiler will come to realize that his literatures and readers require him to go to the considerable effort of preparing these essentially gratuitous comments—if not the ideal of one annotation for each entry, then perhaps selectively, or in groups. If the kind thing to call a bibliography is 'useful', its counterpart for an annotation is 'thoughtful'.

WRITINGS ON ANNOTATION. The definitive discussion is still Savage's *Manual* (1906). While it specifically describes practices of the day in annotating library catalogue cards for general readers, its applicability is much more general, its author sound in his judgements and civilized in his attitudes. Much the same objectives are found in the more recent and summary book by W. C. Berwick Sayers, *First Steps in Annotation in Library Catalogues* (London: Association of Assistant Librarians, 1955). Other discussions of annotation form parts of general bibliography texts, among them Brown (1906), pp. 87–97 (Chapter 6: 'Annotations'); Cowley (1939), pp. 130–42 (Chapter 9: 'Annotations'); Higgins (1941), pp. 23–4; the Library of Congress manual (1954), esp. pp. 56–8, 99–102 (with an excellent list of points to consider), and 115; Robinson (1963), pp. 29–31 in the 1979 ed.; Hale (1970), pp. 103–24, with valuable comments on the implication of annotation on matters of arrangement; and Colainne (1980), a particularly commendable study. The several German articles by Reichardt (1954), Goltz and Waligora (both 1965), I suspect, reflect the influence of the great Russian bibliographer E. I. Samurin. The literature on annotation also extends to include writings on journalistic book reviewing, notable among them John E. Drewry, *Writing Book Reviews* (Boston: The Writer, 1966), esp. pp. 25–30 (Chapter 4: 'The Technique of Reviewing') and pp. 121–34 (Chapter 13: 'What the Experts Say'); Wayne Gard, *Book Reviewing* (New York, London: Alfred A. Knopf, 1927); Llewellyn Jones, *How to Criticize Books* (New York: W. W. Norton, 1928); S. Stephenson Smith, Part I ('Book Reviewing', pp. 3–233) in his *The Craft of the Critic* (New York: Thomas Y. Crowell, 1931), esp. pp. 45–62 (Chapter 4: 'The Book Review'); and Frank Swinnerton, *The Reviewing and Criticism of Books* (London: J. M. Dent, 1939; Ninth Dent Memorial Lecture). Other useful articles include R. Brightman, 'The Reviewing of Scientific and Technical Books: Some First Principles from the Point of View of the Reader,' *ASLIB Proceedings*, vol. 1, no. 2 (August 1949), pp. 125–7; and James Hartley, Alan Branthwaite and Alex Cook, 'Some Problems of Reviewing Research in the Social Sciences', *Journal of Research Communication*, 1 (1978–79), 211–23.

Many of today's major continuing bibliographical services have found it useful to distinguish between abstracts and annotations. [3]

Others have distinguished between descriptive and critical annotations, between digests, summaries, syntheses, and reviews. Such distinctions are likely to be unnecessarily specific for the compiler of bibliographies, in whose finite world the precise differences often overlap. Annotations should be seen as having two broad functions: by providing information that is not part of the citation, they describe and they evaluate. Most annotations do both at once: by telling what is in a work, they help the reader decide whether he needs to look at the work. Exclusively descriptive annotations, such as 'The London edition has illustrations not found in the American edition', can be useful; but exclusively evaluative annotations, such as 'Utter trash' or 'A splendid essay', are usually an impertinence.

CONTENT

What information needs to be included in an annotation? Certain basic internal facts about the text would seem self-obvious. To enumerate them, however, reminds us of how different various writings and literatures are. What is relevant for some cases is impossible or meaningless in others. The purpose of the text; the circumstances of creation; the author's aim; the scope of the subject; the main thesis; in heterogeneous works, a complete or selective listing of the names of specific parts, preferably with their particular authors; the method or plan involved; the special justification for including a text which from its title would appear to be out of scope; the background needed for the reader to understand the book; the viewpoint, slant, prejudices or assumptions; the summary of the plot, short of betraying the ending; the results of any tests, studies or surveys involved; the author's conclusions if they are different from the results; description or evaluation of the presentation (or for audio-visual materials, the performance); the presence of bibliographies, appendices, and useful features included in or supplementary to the main text; collational formulae; comparison with other similar writings; and any other important details that cannot be fitted into the citation, on grounds that the information is not available, or not relevant for all of the entries; characteristics of the ideal copy or the specific physical copy examined—all these are elements that may be appropriate in an annotation.

Remembering that one purpose of an annotation is to enable readers to conclude that they do not really need to go to the original, it is often best to think negatively but to put statements in positive terms: 'Very little on the period before 1846' is better stated as 'Emphasizing the period after 1845'. All the statements in the previous paragraph may be set forth fully in a lengthy annotation; or when space is more limited, as is usual, the compiler selects the most significant. On this basis, a distinction has been made between annotations as 'informative' (explicit and longer, with substantive content, serving possibly in lieu of the full text) or 'indicative' (implicit and shorter, serving mainly to tell the reader whether he needs to consult the full text).

It is understandable in theory that descriptive bibliographers should prescribe annotations as being concerned with content or with history of the production of the book as a physical object; remarks concerning single copies or the history of ownership of copies are inappropriate. On the other hand, it is often extremely useful to know which copies might have manuscript emendations, or which might be bound in leopard-skin, or where Thomas Jefferson's copy is to be found. In the process, as Cowley remarks, the resulting list might be better viewed as a census or a catalogue rather than a bibliography. The compiler has to decide whether the inclusion of such details actually subverts the integrity of the list. One of the virtues of the annotation is its ability to accommodate the supererogatory statement; but it is desirable to avoid it in excess.

External factors are also likely to be relevant in the annotation. It may be important to specify the author's special attributes ('an apostle of the great Professor Schmierkäse'), credentials ('Distinguished Professor at the University of Southern North Dakota'— useful in that it does not imply a bias against freelance scholars and authors), viewpoint ('a distinguished labour mediator who frequently writes on existential theology' or 'a distinguished existential theologian who writes on labour mediation'), or other writings ('author of a leading college textbook in the field'). It may also be useful to place the work on its historical, geographical, ideological, artistic, or some other context, possibly with references to related citations—'based on Ginsberg', 'a condensation of Martin's basic argument', 'takes issue with Scrucci's thesis', 'not as opulent as Bjoerling', 'not as sensitive as Gielgud'. The comparison with other writings in the field, or to other editions of the same basic text (as discussed in Chapter II), may also be seen as properly a part of this statement. The assignment is to bring out the originality of the work, to justify its unique presence in the list. References (in short form) to citations in other bibliographies or discussions in other writings may also be useful.

How explicitly should the compiler express value judgements? He alone can make this decision, having sufficient confidence in his opinion, and surmising how his readers are likely to view his authority. Savage's simple rule—to 'attract the people who can read the books, and discourage those who cannot'[4]—is not as easy as it sounds. The compiler must remember that many neutral statements of fact can carry powerful sanctions. The fanciful examples that appear in the previous paragraph can tell a good deal about the work in question, both to those who are already knowledgeable in the field and to those who wish to be. The compiler thus needs to ask whether any such kinds of statements ought to be collectively suppressed in the interest of objectivity, and to make a policy decision to include or exclude statements that are extremely important but strictly speaking uncalled-for, both general statements ('well written', 'badly proofread', 'interesting but awkward charts', 'undocumented') as well as fairly specific ones ('does not consider Billingsgate's theorem', 'written from a Hungarian angle', 'biased against non-Marxist points of view'). In all circumstances, it should be remembered that complaints are most convincing when they are fair, charitable whenever possible, and well documented.

STYLE

The ideal annotation is as lean as the Oxford clerk's horse; the annotator should thus speak not one word more than is necessary,

and those words should be significant, correct and modest to the
point of moralizing. Since the compiler will be evaluated along
with the texts that are described, a high sense of fairness is called
for, so as to bring out the best in both the literature and the readers.
Scholars are ill served in talking about pot-boilers, for instance,
while popularizers do little credit to their cause in describing
research studies as pedantic: the needs and opportunities are far
subtler than this.[5]

What is expressed clearly in the title certainly does not need to be
repeated. Along the way, the compiler will want to reread his
prose several times, in search of fat to be trimmed. When fewer
than eight or ten words are the rule and perhaps twenty the longest
exception, an annotation can simply be tacked on to the end of the
citation itself. Otherwise it is usually set aside in a separate
paragraph below, inset in its margins and often in smaller type so
that its statements are distinguishable from the citation. In any
event, the more prolix the annotation, however appropriate, the
less conveniently the bibliography can be scanned. For extensive
annotations, it may be useful to establish a fixed sequence of
statements: for instance, contents notes, description, evaluation,
with each given a separate paragraph, rather than grouped
together.

It may also be useful to distinguish two styles of annotation:
complete sentences, appropriate to detailed abstracts or when the
reader is best engaged by a formal prose presentation; and
fragmentary statements, appropriate when there is a specific and
direct message that needs to be communicated. The Library of
Congress manual, which has an excellent discussion of annotations,
uses the terms 'conventional' and 'telegraphic' to distinguish the
two. Full sentences are clearly the more flattering to readers, but
fragments show greater respect for their busyness. In practically all
instances the fragments imply complete sentences. They generally
omit the subject, and in the absence of an active verb imply a
passive one.

It should be remembered that verbs are what give life to all
prose; and a telegraphic style can be efficient and stultifying at the
same time. Some writers on abstracts have proposed that the
choice of verb tenses should be consistent. Strictly speaking, the

past tense is appropriate to what the writer did, the present tense to what the text is, the future tense to what the reader will find. There is nothing wrong in moving from one to the other; it increases contrast, although in excess can lose effectiveness. Most important is that there should be some consistency among annotations, with special circumstances justifying special practices.

Several simple grammatical pitfalls in annotations should also be avoided. Since annotations concern the text itself, it is often difficult to construct concise and relevant sentences that have active verbs and do not have 'this writing' or 'this book' as their subjects; opening fragments of sentences are preferable. It should also be understood that annotations are ultimately personal creations, so that the expressions 'I believe that . . .' and 'I feel that . . .' are not needed. Similarly, it is unnecessary to suggest 'you will find that . . .', although 'The reader will be amused by . . .' may be an admissible inefficiency in a complete-sentence annotation when the objective is to engage the reader. It is perhaps a coincidence that so many annotations read in the course of preparing this text have referred to original findings as having been 'unearthed'. The term 'standard text' is likely to be essentially meaningless and in need of qualification, while such adjectives as 'arcane' are useful mainly for betraying the compiler's biases. Further points can be subsumed in the injunction, 'direct the prose to the intended audience'. Popular readers will be offended and lost because of long words, as scholars will be infuriated by such descriptions as 'handy' or 'a once-over-lightly survey' and by the elliptic fade-out. . . .

On occasion, a direct quotation is preferable to a paraphrase. The point may be particularly important, well formulated, or difficult to put in other words. And of course, one of the best ways to damn an author is to quote him directly. [6]

How does one praise an author? Since laudable quotations are less likely to convey their excellence than awful ones their badness, words like 'important', 'significant' and 'admirable' can often be slipped in. The danger is pretentiousness, which comes from obsequiousness. It does little for either the late Ray Allen Billington or the graduate history student when the latter refers to the former as 'one of the greatest of American historians' or worse, as 'one of the nine greatest'. In expressing both reservations and endorsement, understatement and all possible precision ought to be aimed for; being too wide-eyed is a damning sign of amateurishness, while being exclusively negative is evidence of an axe to grind.

Decisions on citation style are rarely affected by the kinds and levels of readership; but such grounds are important in decisions affecting annotations. Defining a term for the general reader plays down to the audience in the eyes of specialists. It is often possible to bury a dissertation in a statement which the specialist would read over and passively endorse and which the beginner would appreciate ('Discusses the possibility of Spanish influence without taking sides in the controversy').

It is also useful to formulate the vocabulary for annotation with a view to the specific terms being picked up in a subject index to the bibliography. This practice of 'squirreling' is much to be recommended, although it generally requires that the terms be decided on in advance.

It is well to compare annotations toward the end of the project so as to avoid over-used words and to make sure that comparative statements reflect the right priorities of value. It is not necessary, and too time-consuming, to attempt to govern the comparative lengths of annotations, so that important writings get more said about them and minor ones less. Under ideal circumstances, the longest annotation would be no more than three times as long as the shortest; but such rules collapse under many pressures, for instance the listing of contents, long titles to be cited, or detailed points to be quoted.

The handling of adjectives requires caution and understatement, in keeping with Wilbur's observation that adjectives 'are all threadbare, even "seductive" and "intriguing",' while ' "interesting" is . . . the worst of the lot.'[7] It is useful to save words such as 'splendid', 'outstanding', 'monumental', 'breathtaking', 'appalling', and 'disastrous' for truly exceptional instances; and with Roget at hand to distinguish between 'lengthy', 'extended', 'protracted', 'verbose', 'exhaustive' and 'longwinded'. Annotations should also be proofread separately from the citations.

Group annotations are particularly useful and efficient in dealing with minor works, or for purposes of contrasting several texts directly. (This practice is illustrated in the brief essays introducing the lists of 'Major Guides to Bibliographies' at the end of Chapter I and 'Major Style Manuals' at the end of Chapter III.) The annotation may appear after the last citation in a group or it may precede the citations, particularly if it would thereby follow under a section heading and pertain to all of the citations under that heading; or it may fall under the first citation of a group, specifying the titles in consideration. Such an arrangement often calls for special layout by the book designer, indicating when the section begins or ends. One step removed from this practice is the bibliographical essay, a much respected form, notwithstanding the awkwardness of the internal bibliographical citations, which hopelessly clutter a prose text.

NOTES

1. Those who object usually equate annotation with its evaluative rather than its descriptive function. A. W. Pollard's reservations, for instance, largely react to James Duff Brown's assertion that the compiler is obligated to direct readers away from bad literature. Pollard's libertarian instincts emerge clearly in his pronouncement that 'All knowledge is good, and though we have a right, and even a duty, to condemn those who set others to tasks of which the possible result seems incommensurate to the certain labour, on the other hand, where the work is voluntarily and joyously undertaken, what wise man will be so overbold as to fetter the worker's liberty?' See his addenda to Brown, 'Practical Bibliography' (1903), p. 162. His sentiments are echoed, for instance, in Wilfrid S. Bonser's *Romano-British Bibliography* (Oxford: Blackwell, 1964), p. x: 'In no case have I attempted the evaluation of any book or article. . . . Evaluation I hold to be the function and responsibility of the user, and not of the compiler. . . . The user must exercise his judgment, from the date of the work of his knowledge of the writer, as to what is valuable and reliable, also as to what is now obsolete, redundant, or prejudiced.'
2. Lawrence C. Wroth, 'Early Americana', in *Standards of Bibliographical Description* (Philadelphia: University of Pennsylvania Press, 1949), p. 106. Wroth, esp. on pp. 101–6 and 111–13,

offers a particularly powerful testimony in the cause of annotation.
3. For a useful introduction to these concepts *see* J. E. Rush, R.
Salvador and A. Zamora, 'Automatic Abstracting and Indexing',
Journal of the American Society for Information Science, 22 (1971),
260–74, esp. p. 261. I have not seen 'A System Study of Abstracting
and Indexing in the United States' (Falls Church, Va.: System
Development Corporation, 1966; PB 174–249). The literature on
abstracting is itself a large one, often quite technical as well, but
with many relevant discussions for the compiler. A convenient
guide is Robert R. Collison, *Abstracting and Abstracting Services*
(Santa Barbara, Cal.: ABC/Clio Press, 1971). Edward T. Crem-
mins, *The Art of Abstracting* (Philadelphia: I.S.I. Press, 1982) has
many virtues. Also to be highly recommended are the writings on
this subject by Ben H. Weil, perhaps most notably 'Some Reader
Reactions to Abstract Bulletin Style,' *Journal of Chemical Documentation*, 1 (1961), 52–8.
4. Savage, *Manual* (1906), pp. 1–2.
5. Hans Fischer, for instance, makes an admirable distinction
between the annotations of Conrad Gesner—which 'abound in
good will,' as 'he seems anxious to do justice to his authors and
their work'—and the 'clipped, brief, lapidary judgements of the
self-possessed Bernese patrician Albert von Haller.' *See* his 'Conrad
Gessner (1516–1565) as Bibliographer and Encyclopedist', *The
Library*, 5th series, 21 (1966), p. 275. For another telling testimony
to the evaluator's need to consider his own evaluation, *see* the
correspondence between Geoffrey Parsons and Virgil Thomson, as
reprinted under the title of 'The Art of Gentlemanly Discourse' in
John Vinton, *Essays after a Dictionary* (Lewisburg, Penn.: Bucknell
University Press, 1977), pp. 29–77.
6. The importance of brevity in the cause of severe judgment, in
all its gangster-like dispatch, is provocatively implied in
Roland Barthes, 'Power and Cool', in *The Eiffel Tower and
other Mythologies* (New York: Hill and Wang, 1979), pp. 43–5.
7. Susan Warren Wilbur, 'Don'ts for Reviewers', in Llewellyn
Jones, *How to Criticize Books* (New York: W. W. Norton, 1928), p.
185.

CHAPTER V

Organization

The last major consideration before beginning to collect entries is Wilson's fifth specification for bibliographical instruments: 'the frequently extraordinarily complex systems of arrangement or organization'.

Three concepts need to be recognized. *Access*, the main objective, enables the readers to find what is wanted and brings them together with the literature. *Arrangement* is the linear sequence of citations, and nothing more. *Organization* is the overall plan, involving the arrangement, indexes and other features, the conception of the layout of entries, and whatever guidance is given in the introduction. The sum total of these three provides for general access, while their particulars identify what are often called 'search modes'. The basic task is how to organize the content of the list so as to make optimum provisions for access (what information scientists designate 'recall').

WRITINGS ON THE ARRANGEMENT OF BIBLIOGRAPHIES. The landmark statement is Pollard (1909). Other useful discussions may be found in Brown (1906), pp. 66–86; Murray (1914), pp. 25–45; Cowley (1939), pp. 178–94 (Chapter 10: 'Arrangement and Headings'); Esdaile (1931), pp. 277–91 in the 1967 ed. (Chapter 11: 'The Arrangement of Bibliographies'); Hale (1970), pp. 77–128 (Chapters 6 and 7: 'The Arrangement of Subject Bibliographies' and 'The Arrangement of Some Selected Bibliographies', a particularly useful discussion); Robinson (1963), pp. 41–78 in the 1979 ed.

(Chapter 3: 'Arrangement'); Schneider (1934 translation), pp. 140–268 (Part IV, Chapter 3: 'The Arrangement of Titles'); Staveley and the McIlwaines (1961), pp. 69–93 ('Classification: Theoretical Principles'); and Stokes, *Function* (1969), pp. 118–29 (Chapter 5: 'Arrangement of a Bibliography', essentially an outgrowth of the discussions in the author's earlier eds of Esdaile above). I have found very little further that addresses the compiler's needs with much of any precision—least of all on the literature on library classification, characterized as it has been with a concern for the universe of learning, as well as territorial combat between ancient protagonists who sadly display the need for mandatory retirement—but it is possible that I have not known where to look. In any event, hopes rise considerably with the founding of the Classification Society (1964), and in scanning the varied contents of its *Bulletin* (1965–   ). Among the writings cited above, Staveley and the McIlwaines, in the very conception of their book, probably provide the most fertile context for further attempts to address systematically the basic questions of organization of particular bibliographies.

The compiler should first identify every conceivable angle from which a reader might seem to use the list. The best starting point is the list of elements that go into the citations and their component factual information (*see* Chapter 3), to which can be added names and subjects likely to be mentioned in the citations and annotations.

The next task is to organize these elements in terms of their commonalities, in order to establish which of them might become 'points of access'. Of the different statements—author, titles, other names, subjects, dates—which are essential? Which are desirable? Which might best be handled selectively? Which would appear to have no conceivable legitimacy? It is surprisingly easy to adopt a patronizing attitude: some kinds of access may rightly be suppressed, since they are irrelevant or even misleading—a bold, somewhat political pose that ought to be assumed only when the compiler is willing to be attacked by critics. Often there are dimensions that should be left for the reader to discover by reading through the whole bibliography. For example, it is rare for the entries in a list to be accessible through the total number of pages in entries, although it may be important to know that all pre-1940 discussions run to a minimum 150 pages and nothing since 1975 covers more than twenty-five pages—a fact the reader can best understand by reading the entries or possibly from a brief statement in the introduction. Exceptions aside, the compiler's decisions are directed to the objective of access, and they are made in consideration of every imaginable reader—past (a surprisingly useful conception), present, future (a heady prospect, perhaps, but ultimately the object of the exercise).

The next group of decisions is concerned with the various ways of accommodating the points of access:

1. through the basic sequence of the list, since the juxtapositions of entries will convey obvious relationships and imply regressive ones;
2. through cross-references interfiled with the entries, or alternatively, through duplicate entries with abbreviated citations and preferably with specially tailored new annotations;
3. through an index;
4. through special conspectuses, systematic tables, charts, or other features at the end; or
5. through observations in the introduction.

The last four can be deferred for the moment. The first, the matter of arrangement, requires a basic decision: which dimension is the most appropriate for the entries themselves, and how can the sequence of entries best be formulated? What do we arrange, and how do we arrange it? We are talking about the handling of what Bacon calls 'compatibles', in terms of a linear sequence that moves from one place to another so as to avoid the feeling of random disorganization.

Pollard[1] has listed four necessary characteristics of a bibliographic arrangement: it should be *intelligible* so that readers have faith in the compiler's plans, *visible* so that they will always know where they are in relation to where they want to be, *certain* so that the assignment of particular items is convincing and leaves readers as few optional assignments as possible to argue about, and *permanent* so that the arrangement looks good enough to be used in the second edition. All of these Pollard sees as relating to those conditions that are other than 'natural'. He identifies two 'natural sequence' groups—chronology, and 'wholes before parts'—although many others could be equally legitimate in particular situations: 'pure before impure', 'original before copy', 'primary before secondary', or texts themselves before items about the texts. Pollard's lofty agenda makes it clear that no arrangement will be perfect. One decides between alternatives, keeping in mind Pollard's criteria at the theoretical level, and at a practical level, the idiosyncrasies of literatures and the needs of readers.

ALPHABETICAL SEQUENCE

The advantages to an alphabetical arrangement, in Pollard's view, are intelligibility and visibility. But he endorses it only in instances where 'entries are likely to be emulated solely for their own sake'; that is, when there is no need for the arrangement to seek to convey the sense of the subject matter. The sole objective is 'search and find'; the relationship between 'Garfield, James A.' and 'Garibaldi, Giuseppe'—whether full of meaning, inscrutable, or downright bizarre—is in any event irrelevant. [2]

Alphabetical arrangement is assumed usually to cover authors' last names, although there are of course other possibilities. Titles are the implicit arrangement of lists of writings by one person; of serials; of films for which many different contributions are involved; and of popular songs whose composers and lyricists are so often forgotten, some of which might more usefully be arranged by first lines. For official reports the corporate body may be most appropriate. In other words, the decision on arrangement is one of *how* to arrange, and also of *what* to arrange. *What* is arranged is in many ways the counterpart to the library cataloguers' main entry.

Entry rules, of course, are among the rocks on which library cataloguers' perspectives have been foundering for many years. The compiler can deliberate about such matters as much as he wishes; or, giving thanks that his bibliographical world is designed to be less universal and invariable than that of the library cataloguer, he can work out pragmatic solutions, based on what best accommodates Pollard's four criteria, giving preference to the reader's likely first choice.

CHRONOLOGICAL SEQUENCE

The case for chronological sequence of entries is best argued by Lawrence Wroth,[3] beginning with the assumption that 'one of the services of bibliography is the organizing of thought for the purpose of synthesis'. He continues:

> There is . . . a sort of cosmic orderliness about chronology, based, as it is, on the relationship between the earth and the universe or, rather, the earth and the other bodies of the solar system. As the years and the centuries unroll, great cities flourish and decline, nations rise and fall, and changes occur in the mind and heart of man. That development, either of growth or decay, is recorded by the monuments of art and literature which man leaves behind him. Whether the period set forth in the chronological catalogue be one of a century, or a decade, or a single year, the books published provide a picture of events and of the origin and development of the ideas which in that period have inhibited the people or moved them to action. The picture is at once a still and a movie, according to whether one wants to see the period as a whole or in process of growth.

For practical purposes, chronological arrangements are almost invariably based on the date of publication. Dates of creation are known only in rare and unusual instances, and even when known, they are frequently complicated by long gestation periods between the date of conception and the date of termination, with the author's overlapping activities and later reconsiderations of the text further confusing the picture. It is much easier to work with the publication date. An exception would be appropriate in the case of reprints, when the primary aim of the chronology is to suggest the historic changes in content rather than the changing output of the press. A 1724 book reprinted in 1977 usually belongs under 1724 in a subject list, under 1977 in an imprint list. Such arrangements are often labeled 'annalistic', as distinguished from 'chronological' arrangements in which for instance writings are separated which deal with early, middle, late, or other historical periods.

Several problems typically arise with chronological sequence.

First, many topics are characterized by long periods of inactivity, interrupted suddenly by years of prolific production: clumps of entries appear to destroy the purpose of a chronological sequence, although this circumstance is usually significant in its own right. Second, some literatures are characterized by undated materials, among them music, maps and other products of an ephemeral nature or historically printed by engraving and lithography rather than letterpress. Third, and usually the most disturbing, are those books that went through many editions, requiring either a choice between the date of the first edition (which may not be known at all) or of the later edition or editions described (which Pollard prefers). Cross-references are obviously needed, or some alternative to them; and for all these problems, the compiler's imagination has to be called on to work out solutions. The chronological arrangement of the 'Bibliography' in this book may be considered as part of this discussion, for its several examples of the problems (*see* entries 11, 25, 43 and 51, for instance), as well as for the overall advantages of chronological arrangement.

Such obstacles notwithstanding, chronological sequence has the advantage of intelligibility, visibility (even when the dates are buried in the middle of the citation, as discussed in Chapter 4), certainty, and permanence. Its even greater virtue, of course, as Wroth has proposed so eloquently, is that of suggesting the development of the field itself. In dealing with some scientific literatures, the reverse chronological or 'anti-chronological' sequence, with the latest titles first, should not be overlooked; it is rarely as affected as it sounds.

CLASSIFICATION

Pollard, as sage an adviser as he was cautious, boldly describes an arrangement 'by the natural divisions of the subject' as the 'most important, though also the most dangerous'. It is the most important, presumably, because it offers the compiler the opportunity to organize his materials for purposes of pointing up the characteristics of the literature—an ambitious and admirable objective, if perhaps not always necessarily the most important. It is the most dangerous because it tempts the compiler to be carried away by his comprehension of the topic, to show off and over-classify, or otherwise to leave the reader proposing that some different conception would be preferable. (Another way to say this would be to propose that classified arrangements are the most vulnerable to the classic complaint, 'Things are so beautifully organized that I cannot find anything'.) A 'systematic bibliog-raphy' often means a classified list, so that while the origins of the term 'systematic bibliography' seem in fact to be obscure, some writers have assumed it to concern subject classification. Similarly, in French the *catalogue raisonné* is in essence a classified list.

In terms of Pollard's four criteria, the permanence of a classified arrangement depends on the system. Its certainty is intelligible—in fact, its intellectual trappings often border on dogma, and this in its own right can be appealing—notwithstanding the inevitable uncertainties for the compiler in assigning particular citations and for the reader in finding them. Its intelligibility, and even more its visibility, will almost certainly require the amenities of a table of contents, a detailed index at the end, conspicuous section headings, running heads or similar devices on each page and a brief but convincing explanation in the introduction.

What are the options for classification schemes? Irwin's question of library schemes applies equally to bibliographical schemes. 'The vital question is not "Is it a true mirror of reality?" but "Does it work in practice . . .?" '[4] The distinguishing characteristic has to be one of sheer attractiveness. It 'looks good' with a 'right' number of entries in each of its categories so as to make a separate little bibliography of each of them. The way in which the categories relate to each other can often be slightly less than perfectly logical, so long as each category incorporates an intellectually rounded and recognizable unit. This essentially aesthetic dimension will almost certainly be the cause of much misery and hair-tearing for the compiler; in contrast, the agony of the classifier in libraries and for continuing bibliographical projects will usually result more from a rigorous concern for logical relationships. Dissimilar texts, or no texts at all, are acceptable in a library classification category: no matter how 'theoretical' or 'practical' the basic scheme, the category represents the appropriate location, such as may some day be recognized in its full conceptual plenitude. A library classification category looks right when it has a God-given element about it, while a category in a bibliography looks right in terms of the literature being covered.

The list of *delimitations of scope* (*see* Chapter II) may serve the compiler's needs here as well. Separating the entries according to the different media (1) has the advantage of making citation practices much easier and satisfactory; rather than devising one citation style to fit everything, the pattern can be adapted so as to bring out characteristics of the different materials.[5] Separation according to circumstances of production (3) might involve separation of British from Continental imprints, or trade books from official publications; and sometimes such a conception of the 'compatibles' can bring out important relationships very cleanly. Distinguishing according to characteristics of the physical objects (4) does not make much sense until we consider the possibilities that such differences—between tall folios and pocket editions, multi-volume sets and pamphlets, atlases and single maps, 12-inch and 10-inch discs, for instance—may be quite valuable. The notion of bibliographical 'forms' can be full of meaning,[6] suggesting some elements of truth in the notion that 'the medium is the message'. Items in one library (5) may be usefully separated from those more remotely available, possibly even from those not inspected by the compiler. Separation according to language (8) can be helpful in a list directed both to general and specialized scholarly readers. Through a separation according to objective (9), textbooks, propaganda pamphlets, or other special but awkwardly conceived kinds of materials come together into groups; while a separation on qualitative grounds (10) can sometimes allow major works to be emphasized, with the less important ones grouped together in appendix form. These suggest some of the less obvious ways of classifying entries.

By far the most common classification schemes are those that reflect the divisions of subject matter (6), for instance, the content of the chapters in a standard work. They may reflect circumstances of chronology, geography, ideology, biography or combinations of these. Pollard, Esdaile and Robinson give samples that may be worth imitating, whether for authors, historical personages or localities.[7]

Several strong words of advice are in order for those who are considering classified subject arrangements: know the field intimately, be prepared to make alterations for your own special needs, and do not make any commitments until all or nearly all the entries have been collected. Library classification schemes, conceived with the universe of learning in mind, do not conspicuously favour the needs of specialist readers. Imagination, even flashes of inspiration, are needed if the special characteristics of the literature and the needs of the readers are to be brought out. Finally, the compiler should be prepared at the last moment to play a game of solitaire with the entry cards so as to create the greatest number of useful combinations and juxtapositions, leaving the fewest number of Procrustean beds, mixed marriages, dumping grounds, diners with Duke Humphrey, loose ends and odd lots. Next to the tasks of working with citation style and proof reading, this activity is likely to be the most depressing of all to the compiler. Its agonies may be very much worth the trouble.

It is necessary to arrange the categories in relationship to one another, not just to devise categories and fit entries into them. There are several possibilities for the overall conceptions: often systematic and based on logical grounds reflecting the characteristics referred to at the beginning of this section; occasionally alphabetical is better, based on subject categories for which compatible terms can be found. [8] Obviously the task of arranging the categories will be tantamount to the conception of the Table of Contents.

SECONDARY ARRANGEMENT

If the primary arrangement is alphabetically by author, what secondary arrangement will best separate the authors' various writings: alphabetically by title, chronological, by subject, language, form? Within a subject arrangement, do we subdivide by authors or dates? While making decisions, the compiler will find that the considerations on primary arrangement will apply to the secondary arrangement as well. Secondary and even tertiary arrangements become progressively less crucial to the reader's routine consultation of the bibliography; but they remain a reflection of the compiler's ability to convey the integrity of the literature as a whole. The number of entries involved at the secondary level is usually small enough to substitute a special arrangement in individual instances, preferably with a brief note to the reader. In this matter, it may be useful to recall Pollard's observation that chronological sequence might best be used as 'an ultimate or perhaps penultimate, rather than a primary method of classification'. The same may be said of other of the 'natural sequences' mentioned above.

The filing sequence in a bibliography, of course, does not need to be as inflexibly prescribed as that for library card catalogues or computer data bases. Models are always useful, but there may be good reasons to deviate, either through a consistent policy or for a particular group of entries batched together—so long as the practice is clearly understood and logically justifiable. The possibilities of arrangement according to internal elements, for instance, was suggested in Chapter III. In an extended list of writings all by the same author, it looks pedantic to repeat the full name for each entry, and just as bad to simulate the length with an over-long rule. A two-em or three-em dash is enough. The compiler should decide on filing order based on ideas of how the bibliography will function—letter-by-letter suggesting a dictionary or encyclopedia, word-by-word a library card catalogue.[9]

In such matters compilers should be reminded of an intrinsic characteristic—at once both an advantage and a limitation—of bibliographies in general. Unlike card catalogues and computer data bases, lists are typically conceived as self-contained: the prospect of interfiling entries for a supplement or later edition is flattering to consider but not a primary necessity.[10] In return for finality, the compiler gains the special advantages of panoramic presentation. A bibliography, according to a classic dictum of Fredson Bowers, is meant to be read as well as consulted. The reader must find his orientation, which forces one to browse. Scanning is quick, leaves can be turned almost as quickly, and—a happy state that needs to be both appreciated and studied—the reader comes to luxuriate in contexts. Visual mobility encourages discovery, facilitates serendipity and, whether correctly or incorrectly, gives a sense of the totality of the literature. In contrast, the use of the card catalogue is encumbered by visual access to one card at a time, and the slowness with which cards can be fingered and with which eyes adjust to a new visual field; and the computer, in order to work as effectively as possible, needs to be given filing instructions that are as simple, arbitrary and comprehensive as possible. When speaking of visibility Pollard not only identifies a useful consideration for the compiler, but the basic and most important justification for the page in preference to the card or the computer display for bibliographical purposes.

REFERENCES AND INDEXES

It is always possible to duplicate an entry, as one sees in a library's dictionary catalogue: two citations can appear, identical except for the first words, for instance; a report for a corporate body can be listed under both the institutional and personal names. It is usually better, however, to handle matters through cross-references or index entries, asking the reader to go to some extra work but saving considerable space. As a rule, cross-references should be used only when the information is comparable in level to the statements by which the primary arrangement is conceived (for instance, in an author list, 'Twain, Mark, *see* Clemens, Samuel Langhorne'; but not 'Tom Sawyer, *see* Clemens'); otherwise index entries are preferable.

In assembling the index, the compiler who works logically will be attracted to the possibilities of several separate indexes—for instance, one for personal names, another for institutional names, another for concepts—rather than one large alphabetical sequence. A separate list, such as for cities in imprints, can bring out relationships that would be lost in an integrated list. Generally, however, the single alphabet is much easier for the busy reader to consult. When in doubt, the compiler can arrange a sample each way and imagine how the index would be used.

Proper name forms rarely pose any serious problems. All kinds of inconsistencies are possible, but these can be dispatched on the usual bases of precedents, consistency, and anticipated reader habits. The merging of names produces what is sometimes called an 'onomastic' index. Concepts, mentioned in the citations or buried in the annotations, may need a good deal of working over for purposes of consistency and decisions on hierarchical relationships. The subject headings used by library cataloguers and other indexing services should never be adopted uncritically; they will almost certainly be inappropriate to the exact needs of a specialized bibliographical list. For extensive indexes of concepts, some study in the field of thesaurus construction may be useful, and the many writings on indexes are always useful to consult. Ideally the formulation of the index should progress simultaneously with that of the main text, so that entry forms can be standardized as the work progresses and the compiler can find his draft citations in the many different ways that the readers will eventually locate theirs; but such an ideal plan will almost surely prove to be more trouble than it is worth.

WRITINGS ON INDEXING. The literature is immense, as surveyed in Hans Wellisch, *Indexing and Abstracting: An International Bibliography* (Santa Barbara: ABC/Clio Press, 1980). The pragmatic interests of compilers may be addressed in such brief discussions as M. D. Anderson, *Book Indexing* (Cambridge: Cambridge University Press, 1971); Robert L. Collison, *Abstracting and Abstracting Services* (Santa Barbara, Oxford: ABC/Clio Press, 1971), pp. 41–57 ('Indexing'); Sina Spiker, *Indexing your Book: A Practical Guide for Authors* (Madison: University of Wisconsin Press, 1954); or Martha Thorne Wheeler, *New York State Library Indexing: Principles, Rules, and Examples* (Albany: University of the State of New York, 1942). A more extensive programme of preparation might involve either Robert L. Collison, *Indexes and Indexing* (4th revised ed.; London: Ernest Benn; New York: John de Graff, 1972), or G. Norman Knight, *Training in Indexing: A Course of the Society of Indexers* (Cambridge, Mass.: MIT Press, 1969). Among anthologies, Knight's *Indexing, the Art of* (London: George Allen & Unwin, 1979), and Leonard Montague Harrod, *Indexers on Indexing: A Selection of Articles published in The Indexer* (New York, London: R. R. Bowker, 1978) reprint many of the most important essays, many of them taken from *The Indexer* (London, 1958–   ), the official journal of the Society of Indexers. The two Boodson articles (*Harrod*, pp. 271–9 and 280–7) will particularly interest compilers. A. C. Foskett, *A Guide to Personal Names, using Edge-Notched, Uniterm, and Peek-a-boo Cards* (London: Clive Bingley; Hamden, Conn.: Archon Books, 1967; 2nd ed., revised and enlarged, 1970) is largely outmoded in its technology, but still useful for its discussion of some of the problems of logic. As the compiler may need to investigate the highly developed systems used in major abstracting systems, Harold Borko and Charles L. Bernier, *Indexing Concepts and Methods* (New York: Academic Press, 1978) should be consulted, or, more briefly, Charles H. Davis and James Rush, *Guide to Information Science* (Westport, Conn.: Greenwood Press, 1979), pp. 15–31 (Chapter 3: 'Indexing and Classification'). Other brief writings of possible interest include the Library of Congress manual (1954), pp. 107–11, and Nancy A. Blumenstock, 'An Indexer Training Session', *Scholarly Publishing*, 5 (1974), 357–61. The British Standards Institution has issued a standard on *The Preparation of Indexes to Books, Periodicals, and other Publications* (1976; BS 3700), while the American National Standards Institute has issued a standard on *Basic Criteria for Indexes* (Z39.4-1968, revised 1974).

Entry numbers are always preferable to page numbers in an index. They are easier to locate and the compiler can assign them as soon as the entries have been numbered rather than when the pages are finally set for the printer to run off. In theory it is possible to assign preliminary numbers at a fairly early stage of the work, to prepare the index using these numbers and to convert them to final numbers.

The task of organizing a bibliography involves both bright inspirations, and depressing but necessary decisions between nearly evenly balanced alternatives. And while the outcome involves the dull task of shuffling and arranging cards, this task is basic to the very justification for the list being assembled in a final form. The most important point is bibliographical presentation, specifically the differences between page layout, cards in a catalogue, and computer data bases. The latter two forms both have the significant advantage of possible expansion. Furthermore, computer data bases are providing for 'interaction'—for the user to alter the request in the light of previous information. Under the circumstances, the bibliography's special advantages of being laid out on paper need all the more to be appreciated. The linear sequence of entries, supplemented by indexes and other auxiliary features, must be conceived for purposes of suggesting to the reader the basic rationality of the literature itself as well as for purposes of display. Ideally, all readers should be able to open the book to any place, at any time, and at once understand 'what is going on'. In less visionary but no less idealistic terms, the compiler should understand that the organization will be viewed as a coherent intellectual expression in its own right, and an important element in the justification for the list itself.

NOTES

1. Pollard, 'Arrangement' (1909), pp. 172–3.
2. In Tom Stoppard's *Travesties* (London: Faber and Faber, 1975), p. 37, no less an authority than Tristan Tzara is heard to propose that while his friend Cecily the librarian is indeed pretty, her knowledge 'is eccentric, being based on alphabetic preference. She is working her way along the shelves.' Lawrence C. Wroth is clearly in agreement when he proposes that 'no instrument more effective for the fragmentation of thought could be devised . . . than the catalogue arranged upon the alphabetical principle.' See his 'Early Americana', in *Standards of Bibliographical Description* (Philadelphia: University of Pennsylvania Press, 1949), p. 107.
3. *Standards of Bibliographical Description*, pp. 107–8. *See also* Sable (1981).
4. Raymond Irwin, *Librarianship* (London: Grafton, 1949), p. 106.
5. Jacques Barzun and Henry F. Graff, *The Modern Researcher*, 3rd ed. (New York: Harcourt Brace Jovanovich, 1977), pp. 292–3, favour this arrangement, but presumably have in mind supplementary lists at the ends of books and dissertations, rather than separate projects in their own right.
6. Personal experience is reflected in my *English Music Printing, 1553–1700* (London: The Bibliographical Society, 1975), pp. 3–5.
7. Robinson (1963), pp. 54–73 in the 1979 ed.; Esdaile (1931), pp. 350–65, also in later eds; Pollard (1909), pp. 181–7.
8. The strengths and weaknesses of alphabetical subject classification will be particularly clear to compilers who use Besterman's *World Bibliography of Bibliographies*.
9. The difference is easily understood in the simplest of terms. Word-by-word filing is based on the principle of 'nothing before something' (spaces precede symbols so that New York precedes

Newcastle), whereas letter-by-letter filing presumes that 'nothing doesn't exist' (spaces don't count so that Newcastle precedes New York). Complications most inevitably enter the picture, among them abbreviations, hyphens and other punctuation marks, numerals, and the conventions of foreign languages. Dictionaries, most indexes, and reference sources have generally favoured letter-by-letter filing, while library cataloguing has generally favoured word-by-word. Among the major library practices, that of the British Library is described in its *Filing Rules* ('Final draft', 1979). American practice involves either the *ALA Filing Rules*, prepared by its Filing Committee of the Resources and Technical Services Division (Chicago: American Library Association, 1980), or John C. Rather and Susan C. Biebel, *Library of Congress Filing Rules* (Washington: Library of Congress, 1980). *See also* Ernst Kohn, 'The New German Filing Rules', *International Cataloguing*, 7 (1978), 7–10. Computer filing practices are obviously changing many of the established practices, so that one of the best recent surveys of variant practices, by Fred Ayres, is appropriately entitled, 'It's Not as Easy as ABC,' *Catalogue and Index*, 54 (Autumn 1979), 1–3, 8.

10. The battlefield on which two different plans for re-numbering have now been tested, and a valuable case-study for the compiler, is the second ed. of Donald Wing's *Short-Title Catalogue of Books...*, *1641–1700*. While the entry numbering practices have been the most conspicuous grounds for controversy, the over-riding problem involves the simplistic approach to sequential arrangement, appropriate perhaps to a corpus of several hundred author entries, but not to a corpus of the size and complexity here.

CHAPTER VI

Collecting Entries

THE COMPILER'S RESOURCES

The compiler starts planning the task of collecting entries with a survey of the resources needed and available. *Money* is always foremost among the resources. It is likely to be in short supply, but essential mostly for inexpensive supplies such as cards and stationery. When funds are available, it is always possible and often helpful to commit them for secretarial transcription of dictated entries, photocopying, access to online data bases, printed cards, parking and transportation.

A more important resource is *time*, which the compiler should analyse in three ways: (1) the kind of time—prime time or off-hours—at home, in a library or elsewhere—extended periods or time in bits and pieces; (2) the total number of hours likely to be available and needed; and (3) the final deadline, comfortable and ideal or oppressive and drastic. It is gratifying how much can be accomplished in bits and pieces, in random moments and in passing thought. [1] As for estimates and projections for planning purposes, the most reliable guideline is probably Parkinson's Law, 'work expands to accommodate the amount of time allowed for it'. The same law expands to postpone deadlines, and to legitimize their postponement, so that it is safe to see the final deadline as existing about two-thirds of the way through the calendar, in anticipation of the predictable Murphy's Law, 'if anything can go wrong, it will'. There is never enough of any kind of time, and when there is, it should be committed to an improvement of quality rather than expansion of scope.

The compiler's *expertise* is the third resource. While it cannot be underestimated, even recognized authorities will attest that much of it is developed in the course of the work, admittedly at considerable detriment to efficiency and with some personal awkwardness to the compiler. One must agree in large part with Wilbur's dictum, 'Unless you have some knowledge of the subject or some angle upon it, the chances are that you won't be able to write anything that will be of value to the reader who seeks your guidance in his selection of books'. [2] But there is much work to be done; and there are energetic and able compilers around who want and need to benefit from and contribute to the public stock of knowledge. They should not necessarily be discouraged, only forewarned and advised. It is well for the humble tiro to be reminded that expertise is relative and not absolute; and no subject is finite enough to admit of experts who know and remember everything within its compass.

To argue between the expertise of a subject specialist and the librarian's expertise in working with the bibliographical record is an exercise usually undertaken to glorify one at the expense of the other. Admittedly, most subject specialists are either deficient in their abilities to use a library, or self-taught. More important, they can easily be encumbered by the orthodoxies and awed by the boundaries of their academic disciplines. Those subject specialists who compile bibliographies are usually either the best—who can do anything they please and welcome the overview which a bibliographical project can provide—or the worst, who, lacking ideas but needing something to do, construct monuments to yesterday's intellectual values. On the other hand, it is mischievous nonsense to propose that librarians, information specialists and other generalists who pride themselves in seeing forests rather than trees can come up with lists that, however useful, are anything but incomplete and intellectually flawed. Occasionally they will dig up citations or perspectives that the established specialist would overlook, avoid, even suppress; but there is almost always an awkwardness and imprecision of communication, if not significant errors and omissions. Ultimately the question comes to be addressed by logic that is oddly circular: the evidence of a well-conceived and well-executed bibliography is also evidence that the compiler is a respectable bibliographical specialist in his own right, formal academic credentials or other forms of recognition notwithstanding.[3]

Subject expertise is varied in its components; and it is impossible to separate a knowledge of specifics from a knowledge of sources, since the basic tasks so largely consist of the location and verification of facts. Names (correctly spelled), dates (understood in relation to each other), places (their importance in relation to the subject), ideas and attitudes (their implication on matters of scope and arrangement), historical events—all of these would seem to fit under the rubric of subject expertise.[4]

Bibliographical expertise, on the other hand, seems more a matter of training in work habits: efficiency and discipline in correct transcription; knowing when to stop and when to digress; a commitment to service to others, and some knowledge of what this involves and how it can be accomplished; and finally, that awesome, essentially vague, but none the less fundamental skill known as 'search strategy'. To these must be added a knowledge of languages, if not the ability to speak, write and listen in all of them, at least enough to read citations and survey strategically the texts themselves. Mistakes are inevitable; and a well-selected and convenient shelf of general and subject-area reference books should be seen as a necessary adjunct for even the best compiler.

Access to materials is the fourth resource. Major library collections are essential; the compiler who does not have them nearby will need to plan for extensive travel, for visits to aunts with spare bedrooms in library communities. In a limited way, correspondence can be called on. Usually, however, the compiler will need to examine some documents best seen in the original at distant libraries—not so objectionable, since interesting things can often be learned from the way in which the topic has been variously treated by other libraries, in matters of acquisition, classification, reader access and processing of physical documents. It should be appreciated that most general libraries are inevitably highly imperfect institutions for any one particular subject specialist.

Library classification schemes and subject headings, having of necessity been conceived in the context of the universe of learning, have only a limited usefulness, the former for instance when browsing and stack access are permitted, the latter for purposes of turning up the odd lead. A knowledgeable colleague on the staff of the library is of great value, while slow but predictable delivery can be tolerated and planned for if the library has the necessary materials.

WRITINGS ON RESEARCH PROCEDURES. Compilers' descriptions of their work—notably among them, Gaselee (1932), Baer (1954), Bercaw, Bourton and Harlow (all 1956), Walford (1960), Besterman (1974), Bryer (1978), and Evans (1983)—often provide helpful advice in procedural matters interlaced with the basic apologia. *See also* Sam Duker, 'The Joys and Woes', *RQ*, 10 (1970) 15–17. The compiler may also benefit from the injunctions and viewpoints expressed in general handbooks for researchers, among them Richard D. Altick, *The Art of Literary Research* (New York: W. W. Norton, 1963), esp. chapters 5–7 (pp. 118–80), and Jacques Barzun and Henry F. Graff, *The Modern Researcher* (3rd ed. New York: Harcourt, Brace, Jovanovich, 1977). Gilbert J. Garraghan, *A Guide to Historical Method* (New York: Fordham University Press, 1957) offers procedures that are well spelt out in chapter 6, 'Mechanical Aids to Research' (pp. 124–40); as does, in even greater detail, Earle Dow, *Principles of a Note System for Historical Studies* (New York; London: Century, 1924). K. E. Hunt, *Collecting, Storing, and Using Information* (Oxford: n.p., 1962) deserves a wider audience than it has probably received, while George Watson, *The Literary Thesis: A Guide to Research* (London: Longman, 1970) is well worth the hour or so it takes to read. Staveley and McIlwaine (1967) may prove especially valuable for specialists who need to investigate foreign terrains, while other useful perspectives will often turn up in highly general handbooks like John C. Almack, *Research and Thesis Writing* (Boston: Houghton Mifflin, 1930), esp. chapter 9 ('The Library and Thesis Writing', pp. 223–51); William A. Bagley, *Facts and How to Find Them* (7th ed., London: Pitman, 1964), esp. chapters 17–18 ('Using the Books: Note-Taking', pp. 105–16, and 'Some Other Sources of Information', pp. 117–24); Arvid James Burke and Mary A. Burke, *Documentation in Education* (New York: Teachers College Press, 1967); Foskett (1977); J. Edwin Holmstrom, *How to Take, Keep, and Use Notes* (London: Aslib, 1947; Aslib Pamphlets, 1.); Lucyle Hook and Mary Virginia Gaver, *The Research Paper* (New York: Prentice-Hall, 1969); Kenneth W. Houp and Thomas E. Pearsall, *Reporting Technical Information* (3rd ed. Beverly Hills, Cal.: Glencoe Press, 1977), esp. chapters 3–4 ('Finding your Way in a

Library', pp. 13–35, and 'Gathering Information', pp. 36–59); John H. Mitchell, *Writing for Professional and Technical Journals* (New York: John Wiley, 1968), esp. chapters 2–3 ('Data Collection and Correlation', pp. 9–71, and 'Data Selection and Arrangement', pp. 72–88); B. E. Noltingk, *The Art of Research* (Amsterdam: Elzevier, 1965), esp. chapter 5 ('How?', pp. 103–31); John Edward Seyfried, *Principles and Methods of Research* (Albuquerque: University of New Mexico Press, 1935; Bulletin 269, Education Series, vol. 9, no. 1), esp. chapter 5 ('The Library and its Use', pp. 47–56); Alden Todd, *Finding Facts Fast: How to Find out What You Want and Need to Know* (Berkeley, Cal.: Ten Speed Press, 1979); Frederick Lamson Whitney, *The Elements of Research* (3rd ed. New York: Prentice Hall, 1950), esp. chapter 4 ('The Evaluation of Previous Research', pp. 97–108); and Cecil B. Williams and Allan H. Stevenson, *A Research Manual* (New York: Harper & Bros., 1940), esp. chapters 2 and 5 ('The Library as a Place for Doing Research', pp. 12–28, and 'Notes and Note-Taking', pp. 51–65).

FILE ORGANIZATION

Two prototypical plans are available for recording entries. The *commonplace book*, a blank ledger, notebook or other sequential record provides for entries and other data to be copied as they turn up. The book is conveniently portable, less bulky than a pack of cards and always present in its entirety. There is no danger of individual slips being lost, although of course one may lose the whole book. When a considerable amount of information is available on one page, the compiler can scan easily and often detect regressing relationships. The book is also a record of the growth of the compiler's conception, enabling one to look back on the progress. Indexing is, as Garraghan so convincingly puts it, 'not wholly unsatisfactory'; and through roughly sketched attempts alternative arrangements of the entries can be considered. In contrast, the *card file* has the great advantage of re-arrangement. Inexpensive photocopying today makes it easy to convert a card file to a book layout by 'shingling' the cards; whereas a book can be converted to cards only through the much more cumbersome process of clipping and pasting. To be sure, the fingering of cards, and adjusting the vision to the succession as it appears, are immeasurable inefficiencies too easily overlooked. While a few compilers still prefer the commonplace book, most prefer some kind of slip or card, and Beatrice Webb was particularly outspoken in the matter. [5]

The slips may be of any size. While 3 × 5 inches always seems to come to mind first because of library practices, larger sizes (127 × 177 mm, 152 × 229 mm, or even 210 × 295 mm whole sheets, sometimes folded in two) are preferred by many experienced compilers. The larger sheet provides space for more ample notes, but a decided disadvantage when the compiler, seeing the blank space, feels impelled to write something that may or may not be useful. If 3 × 5 cards are used, it may be worthwhile to order Library of Congress cards or to photocopy local library catalogue cards. Except when hundreds of items are involved, however, the inconvenience of placing and awaiting an order or doing the photocopying probably offsets the time spent in transcribing, along with the proof-reading needed to ensure correctness. The paper will need to be heavy card stock only when the file is likely to be handled and reorganized a number of times or expanded over the years; otherwise, ordinary writing stock is entirely adequate. [6] Colour-coding of the cards or slips—yellow for French, pink for German or blue for government documents—may make life more exciting for the compiler but is likely to be more trouble than it is worth. The common practice is to write lengthwise, probably because the visual field is more comfortable; but there is nothing wrong with writing crosswise, which is likely to be preferable when the slips are large and the notes extensive.

Depending on the compiler's resources and needs, it may be appropriate to introduce the computer (1) at the outset—and this will require the materials being cited to be used alongside the inputting terminal; (2) after each entry is in a final or near-final form, so as to involve merely the transfer of entries from slips through re-typing; (3) at various stages, so as to allow for the optimum use of computers in revision and expansion of data, but so as also to require the compiler either to remember, or provide a means for the computer to remember, the nature of the incompleteness; or (4), probably most likely for modest-sized but intellectually intricate projects, not at all.

How then should the working file be organized? There are endless possibilities ranging from the rigid to the casual, from the detailed to the simplistic. Two over-riding considerations need to be accommodated: *process* and *access*. When computers are used, with planning it is possible to reconcile the two; when computers are not used, the compiler must choose between them. For the present discussion, it is easier and more useful to think in terms of the latter of these prospects.

The slips, for instance, may be arranged in one sequence according to what the compiler is most likely to remember best — which may or may not be the filing element in the final list. Usually it will be the name of the author, although it could conceivably be the date, subject, or form classification. Arbitrary and provisional decisions will be needed for anonymous works, undated items or other ambiguous matters. At least the compiler will be able to find any item as needed. It follows that the fewest number of cards should be out of order at any time.

Alternatively, the slips may be arranged in categories for the steps in the process. There are considerable advantages to separate files, for example, for (1) entries that are known to exist but not yet located; (2) entries with local call numbers not yet inspected; (3) entries not in local libraries; (4) entries examined, but with some detail in need of further attention; (5) entries in their final form; and perhaps (6) miscellaneous snags. The number of such categories could be fewer or conceivably somewhat — but preferably not too much — greater, depending on the project. Using the six categories above, the compiler would need to look through six files in order to find a particular entry, although personal memory would likely reduce the number of searches.

There are obvious advantages to either plan; but keeping in mind the size of the list, the compiler's memory, the complexity of both the materials and the process, and the tendency of fluid categories to break down, merge, and subdivide, arrangement by access is usually preferable. Processing can be accommodated by signalling the cards. Signalling can be done with marks in an upper corner, by the venerable paper clip or by coloured tabs for complicated systems. Such tabs do not get lost as often as one might fear, but to set the compiler's already persecuted mind at ease, staples or tape tabs may be used. All such attachments are apt to tear the slip, especially those on thin paper stock. Notched cards, or as Stokes suggests, coloured slips, are more foolproof but also more cumbersome. The slips should be pulled for the processing operation itself, but so long as the compiler is diligent about pulling them at the last possible minute and refiling them as soon as possible, there is no need to design a sub-system for indicating those cards that are 'in process' and temporarily out of place.

There is always the temptation to reorganize the whole file, to shuffle slips in search of new perspectives. It is fun, at least at first, and sometimes enlightening; it is also a great waste of time, especially when the list runs to more than one hundred entries. The compiler, having been excited by Webb's essay, needs to be reminded that his product will be a list, not an essay: the fun of shuffling is for the reader. The self-indulgent compiler who needs to play solitaire should get a deck of cards; and the poor compiler who justifies hours of classifying and reclassifying as a special form of love-making needs a good holiday. The compiler will continually need to consider the final arrangement and how it will look, but its principles usually come better into focus when abstracted through a note pad, leaving the cards as they were. In time the working arrangement evolves into the final arrangement: where the compiler looks becomes the place where he expects the reader to look.

In addition to the main file of entries, it is useful for the compiler to maintain an auxiliary 'side file' of miscellaneous information. Something of a mixture of grab-bag and personal diary, this file can usefully include accessory memoranda such as unusual spellings and words to be looked up in a dictionary when one is handy; reminders of places to check; even matters totally irrelevant to the project; ideas for organization of the list; terms, concepts and well-turned phrases to be fitted into the introduction; attempts at a list of abbreviations or *ad hoc* decisions toward such a list; or details on how long certain operations have required. Surveying this record, from time to time, and near the end of the project, often turns up forgotten topics and new relationships, even alas, additional matters to be investigated. Such a file will probably be small enough to require no special organization; if the file grows out of hand, it can perhaps be arranged by priorities, the most important items at the front, some notations combined or discarded. The file can also be kept in book form, as something of a diary.

SOURCES

It is now time to return and pick up the first of Wilson's specifications, called 'domain'; that is, 'the set of items from which the contents of the work, the items actually listed, are selected and drawn'. Wilson's concept leads to important perspectives and insights, although it can be rather misleading if conceived too literally by the compiler. Specifically, it may suggest that the task is one of working primarily with citations, rather than with writings as reflected in citations.

Compilers may easily be misled into concluding that their topics are comprehended within something less than the totality of the world's bibliographical record. They always are, of course: the problem is one of knowing where, and any list that mis-guesses is by definition an inferior list. Some bibliographies wisely and thoughtfully acknowledge their limited domain, and we use them and often admire their craftsmanship in other respects. But we save our deepest admiration for those works that extend their authority—often in gratuitous, even in erratic and always in imperfect ways—so as to imply an awareness of the universe of our bibliographical record.

Library and information scientists today recognize and study Bradford's law, which for present purposes proposes a point of diminishing returns from the various sources consulted, the first group of sources yielding most of the references to the literature, the next group far fewer, the last group so few as scarcely to be worth the searching effort. [7] 'Any abstracting or indexing service that ignores Bradford's law in attempting to realize the myth of complete coverage,' according to Garfield, 'does so at its great financial peril.' [8] So of course does the compiler. But the peril needs to be addressed, since the process of doing so is what yields the unusual references and new perspectives, promises the respect and continued considered consultation by the intended readers and thus often justifies the bibliography in the first place. To the extent that the fundamental differences between librarians and scholars may ever be defined, here is probably one of the major bases for doing so. It may also account for the low esteem in which the scholarly efforts of librarians, determined and delimited by their institutional responsibilities, are so frequently held by specialist scholars, whose over-riding responsibilities are to the advancement of learning directly.

Obviously the concept of domain will be invaluable, meanwhile, for planning purposes, so long as it is viewed as something that helps in organizing procedures without excluding options. It may be true that many useful lists grow out of a narrowly delimited domain, but these are best passed off humbly as reading lists rather than glorified with the name of bibliographies. The bibliographies that command respect are those that give evidence of considerable hunting over an awesomely wide domain, not only for entries but also for the hunting grounds themselves.

Wilson's conception is also useful for purposes of bringing out the important distinction between failures and 'negative successes'. [9] The difference lies in the certitude of the latter. The former calls for the searcher to report, 'I can't find what I'm looking for', and nothing more than this. The implication is that the object might be in another location which the searcher has not investigated and perhaps not even thought of—a situation that arises frequently in lists that are finely classified or with ambiguous entry elements. In contrast, a 'negative success' enables the searcher to report, 'I can't find what I'm looking for; and furthermore, there can be no question that it's not there at all'. Many sources will yield no new materials, and it is indeed valuable for this information to be specified in the introduction to the bibliography for the limited needs of the reader in search of the literature itself or for the compiler of another list. Unfortunately, some yield nothing at the early stages of work, but as the scope comes into focus and changes, are worth returning to. Many sources will duplicate each other in their contents, so that the bibliographer may find it useful to compare and evaluate the differing contents and style of two citations of the same entry for purposes of developing still different statements particularly appropriate to the special readers of the list in question.

Where then does one start? The answer: everywhere at once, ideally in several places at once so as to give the feeling of immersion in the topic. There is usually a wide range of sources, mostly general in character, to be used to get us into the subject; and the wider the range, the better. These include library catalogues, encyclopaedia articles, biographies and bibliographies of the great names, reference books, computer data bases, general writings, and textbooks, works both in the field itself and in the various larger areas of which it is a part. There will surely be considerable duplication of titles, which can help the compiler size up the literature as well as the sources. These kinds of sources being the ones to which the compiler may return several times before the list is completed, they are also the logical place to take tentative first steps.

Central and specific sources should be consulted before proceeding to a different kind of source, which is typically (1) vast, (2) time-consuming to use, and (3) likely to yield only a few entries. Such sources are difficult to specify for all projects except through these three conditions. They may be national bibliographies, other massive records with poor indexes or none at all, or union catalogues in instances where a long list of authors must be searched. The general strategy, of which this practice is the most common instance, is to undertake extensive major unified efforts only when the general objective is clearly in mind.

One of the most promising of all sources consists of the footnotes, references, and bibliographies in the writings in the field. As the compiler examines texts for the purposes of preparing their citations, he should also survey them for other references. The process begins with the table of contents; jumps over to strategic passages of text; takes special note of the acknowledgments, the footnotes, and other suggestions of sources; and along the way includes a careful examination of the index. For articles that do not include these features in self-contained sections, the whole text will need to be scanned. The search for citations and the examination of texts will usually proceed simultaneously and any attempt to separate the two processes will probably prove to be counter-productive. Similarly but for slightly different reasons, Father Garraghan's rule no. 123 for historians—work first on primary material, then on secondary—is likely to be less than beneficial to compilers, except where derivative texts may need to be evaluated in terms of their models. [10]

Bibliographies of bibliographies such as Besterman, and narrative 'guides for the researcher' [11] might seem a useful place to start. They often lead to promising and obscure sources, but are probably best scheduled for examination between one-third and two-thirds of the way through the projected time schedule. They will likely prove useful only after the precise relevance of their entries can be sized up, and their alternative subject categories explored. On the other hand, leaving them to the very end could result in a last minute deluge of entries.

Subject headings in library catalogues are usually a highly unsettling means of access. Instances of major writings being left out and minor or irrelevant ones included are so common as to leave us with the disturbing conclusion that subject access to the world's literature is one of the major failings of modern library cataloguing. The compiler will use general library subject headings but should not expect them to be comprehensive; subject access schemes tailored to the more finite needs of particular subject specialities are likely to be much more convincing and usable. One useful way to 'get inside' a subject heading system is to identify the headings assigned to a particularly major work in that field, then to look under those headings, a tactic that librarians sometimes refer to as 'triangulation'.

Among the sources that compilers might overlook, special notice should be paid to the announcements and catalogues of booksellers and publishers. Antiquarian booksellers in particular are often impressively learned—they have to be if they are to make a living. Their annotated entries, and their conversation as well, are likely to prove invaluable to the compiler.

In dealing with current materials, the compiler will want to find a way for announcements, stock lists in his subject areas, and other such materials to pass through his hands. Acquisitions librarians, bookshops, and other recipients of bulk mailings may need to be approached. Finding one's way from all such citations to the documents themselves can sometimes be a major task, which will make the compiler all the more appreciative of what librarians have achieved over the last half-century in implementing the injunction that 'no book should be out of reach'.[12]

The importance of ephemeral documents should not be overlooked. Libraries, typically and perhaps necessarily, ignore, discard or relegate to the vertical file a wide range of items too insignificant to deserve proper cataloguing: information leaflets, reading lists, manufacturer's announcements and catalogues, promotional literature, dust jackets for books (a particularly rich but problematical source for annotations),[13] flyers, pamphlets, propaganda, handouts for lectures, and the like. Such documents may be part of the sub-culture of bibliography; and while they themselves may not be appropriate to the scope of a list, they are an invaluable source of information that ought not to be forgotten.

Among the most valuable sources of information are those leads a compiler receives personally from colleagues, as part of what is known disparagingly as the 'grapevine' or the 'old-boy network', and flatteringly as the 'invisible college'. The world of scholarship may be vast and forbidding, but it is not conspicuously unfriendly and is anything but unsociable. The legendary monsters do exist, scholars of great stature who enjoy devouring other creatures, including friendly little compilers. But for each such person there are ten others who are happy to share leads and positively love to give advice. Often they welcome an obscure reference in return. Recognized scholars being generally those who have shown ability to synthesize rather than store facts, the specific references they offer are likely to be the ones found in their books published ten years ago; but their advice in matters of scope, organization and annotation is likely to be particularly useful. For specific references, go instead to the protégés and graduate students. Of particular importance is information on work in progress. Here it is that the compiler can confirm that there is not some other person working on the exact same list, or can learn about a complementary project with which co-operation would be beneficial. Communication with specialists is also important for purposes of providing more precise concepts in the annotations. Generally the effect is to smooth out the critical statements or make them more sympathetic, notwithstanding the occasional opportunity to display one's great finesse with the rapier. A compiler's work clearly improves in quality as it comes to be refined by his acquaintance with the trends, internal conflicts, pressures, events and politics of the field itself. The compiler, being an 'insider' by the time the list is issued, ought to expect his final-published work to be a part of that history.

RESEARCH ACTIVITIES

Once the searching for titles is underway, the compiler is likely to be a driven and tormented creature, enemy to his friends and to himself, exhilarated to the point of being a bore, and single-minded often to the detriment of the project. The agony, bad manners, and frenzy can be passed off as part of the price of any respectable achievement, but the single-mindedness calls for some coaching and preparation. The compiler's concentration on the literature, for instance, can easily cause the needs of the intended readers to be overlooked—a matter that deserves frequent reminders.

The bibliographical list is a highly concentrated statement, with a high density of detail. The compiler must, therefore, be particularly attentive to commitments of time and energy for purposes of insuring the accuracy of his statements. In planning the work, he should look for ways of saving steps, for efficiencies that might be achieved through *batching*. The simplest of all possible procedures, for instance, would call for each entry to be processed from beginning to end one at a time: once the reference is located, find the book, examine it, prepare the entry, then go on to the next reference. Such a procedure would of course be enormously wasteful, although it will probably take place, particularly near the end of the project. We gain much by batching—copying out a number of references, searching a number of call numbers in one alphabet, and examining the books as a group, going from library to library, deferring to a 'snag' category those 'in the bindery' or otherwise unavailable.

Other considerations on the sequence of consulting sources may or may not be worthwhile; for instance, beginning with the current literature and working backward to get some sense of the changing concepts as reflected in subject-heading systems, beginning with English-language materials and progressing to less-well-known languages, or dealing first with the monographic literature before proceeding to periodicals and other forms. Such is part of the essence of the developing speciality being addressed by librarians and information specialists today, known as 'search strategy'. Assuming their ultimate commitment to finality, authority and painstaking completeness, compilers should feel no guilt about doing the easy jobs first, since the faster the file grows at first the lesser the prospect of disastrous surprises later on.

WRITINGS ON SEARCHING FOR ENTRIES. Many of the texts listed in the bibliographical note 'Writings on Research Procedures' earlier in this chapter will provide ample guidance appropriate to the limited needs of compilers. For a bibliographical essay on the specialized literature on searching in general, with special emphasis on computer searching, *see* Marcia J. Bates, 'Search Techniques,' *Annual Review of Information Science and Technology*, 16 (1981), 139–69. Three articles that may be of special value to compilers, all in the same journal, are F. S. Stych, 'Decision Factors in Search Strategy,' *RQ*, 12 (1972), 143–7; Frederick Holler, 'Toward a Reference Theory,' *RQ*, 14 (1975), 301–9; and James Benson and Ruth Kay Maloney, 'Principles of Searching,' *RQ*, 14 (1975), 316–20. Weitzel (1962) delves into the rudiments of systematic method, with special attention to early and continental books.

Batching results in an organization by process. The five basic steps are essentially identification, location, examination, description and completion. These steps can be placed on a flow chart, necessarily with ample opportunities for arrows that return to earlier steps; a few 'loops' are helpful as a means of double-checking. The five steps frequently merge and subdivide as the work progresses, along unpredictable lines and in unpredictable ways. Since there are so many relevant factors—the size of the list, the memory of the compiler, and the detail of the description—the compiler needs mostly to be alert to the values of batching operations. As more than one person comes to be involved, fixed procedures become absolutely necessary. And even for small check lists prepared by compilers with infallible memories, a system of signals on the slips will be useful in recording those steps that have been completed, as well as unusual ones that need to be done.

There are obvious limitations to batching. It may be good thinking to plan the New York trip near the end of the project, but it is predictable that another reference to a copy available only in New York will turn up the day after the compiler returns home from New York. Loose ends may be most efficiently organized in one huge batch; but as detail accumulates and time passes, we tend to forget which ends are loose and what is loose in them. Working against the very idea of efficiency, of course, is the useful 'pilot study', in which one segment of the list is pursued independently, so as to give some idea of the likely problems, schedule, and prospects of the whole project. It is also psychologically useful along the way to plan some changes of pace, for purposes of sustaining the freshness of attitude and allowing for the most productive interrelationships of the various activities. Card filing and text transcription may be among the less demanding activities, but they call for no less accuracy and thought than the more stimulating tasks of scanning an index or evaluating a text: they should never be performed when the head is swimming with ideas, or at 1:30A.M.

The compiler also needs to decide *how much* and *what to write down*. Including too much is a waste of time; but even more time is wasted if it is necessary to return to the item to add something omitted the first time. Locations and call numbers should always be included, even though they may not appear in the final citation. As a general rule, the less conveniently accessible an item, the fuller should be the notes. Fullness of information is not the same as avoiding abbreviations, since terse information is usually just as clear as the full form ('p.' conveys as much, for instance, as 'pages'). Obviously there should be no fixed rules, and some wastefulness at first ought to be expected. The extent and scope of the annotation is particularly vexing.

Advice on note-taking quickly becomes sheer pomp. One source, for instance, threatens us with 'inadequate and very probably misleading' results when our 'work has been impressionistic, superficial, or hasty rather than rapid'. The point beyond which rapid work becomes hasty, however, is not identified. Furthermore, it is also possible to be slow and sloppy at the same time. The important discipline involves control of watchfulness, not of speed. An almost passionate, desperate, cruel and inefficient search for anything that might possibly go wrong is the only means to achieving accuracy. Curiously, keeping this search to the fore stops the mind from wandering, a serious problem when bright people do dull jobs like transcribing. Above all, the compiler must assume the habit of double-checking every entry, and returning after some break in time to triple-check every third entry, in time every tenth or thirtieth, as the absence of errors allows. It is not a bad practice to copy a citation from a secondary reference and then verify it against the original, since it is usually easier and always more pleasant to catch other people's errors than one's own. Every transcription of an entry will need to be checked against its immediate model: the practice of saving all of the interim steps by verifying only the last transcription—intended for the printer—against the earliest, ought to work in theory, but in practice never seems to. As a general rule, the longer the time between transcription and checking, the more likely the prospect of finding an error.

Rather than transcribe entries by hand, the compiler may use *photocopying* or *dictating* equipment. Photocopying can become expensive, but whole entries can be more leisurely consulted for annotations, while even single pages provide an authoritative source for proof-reading. Dictating equipment can be usefully employed in areas where silence is not mandatory; even when the compiler has no secretary and needs to transcribe the text himself, it can save precious time, since time at one's desk is generally easier to come by than time in a library. Practice in work with dictated entries is of course essential, since the fear of error in using an oral rather than a written record is partly justified. The prospect of error or misunderstanding can be minimized by the simple expedient of reading the information twice, once for transcription and a second time for checking. In reading a citation, names and unusual words should be spelled out, letter by letter; numbers and punctuation will need to be clearly signalled. The conversational nature of the process can have the added advantage of allowing the compiler more freedom, as he constructs annotations more tentatively at the time of inspection. Bourton suggests an appropriate rate of twenty entries an hour, roughly twice the speed of manual transcription, but with several special complications to consider. [14]

In handling materials, it should be remembered that some texts will need to be returned to a number of times, and are ideally kept near the compiler's desk. Presumably with professional journals in mind Bateson comments, 'The fact of possession—preferably paid out of one's own pocket—guarantees a much closer attention to all the separate articles and reviews, whether they are of one's own special period or not.'[15] Other materials can perhaps be noted once and then forgotten, although large-scale photocopying is cheap and the resulting convenience may be worth the cost. As a general rule, the more central the writing to the topic, and the more remote and evasive the copy, the more justifiable the photocopy.

Desk space for the compiler is hard to measure, since projects go through stages. Comforting as a library carrel can be, the space and facilities are only rarely appropriate to the needs of the project. At times vast space will be desirable so the materials can be spread out; at other times, the compiler will be running from one building to another, from one corner of the library to the opposite corner. At other times a typewriter will be invaluable, then a telephone, now twenty-five reference books or space for conferences. Under such circumstances, the assigned carrel is at best a symbolic rather than functional convenience.

Distant communications for books and information should be batched whenever possible, and handled at an early opportunity; leaving them for an impending deadline has in more than one instance been disastrous. What might appear as batching will probably be more easily handled as several separate inquiries at the other end. In such matters, it is worth remembering the advantages of the telephone.

The practice of moving back and forth from references to copies is an engrossing experience, which demands ingenuity as it turns up its share of surprises. As the compiler delves deeper into the literature, he finds his attitudes changing: yesterday's long shot proves to be today's essential operation, and vice versa.

The file will usually grow erratically by plateaus, with sudden increments of a dozen or even one hundred entries at a time. This is a reflection neither on the mischief of the topic nor on the compiler's competence. The achievement of past writers is usually much more extensive than was at first apparent; the deployment of documentary evidence is much more unpredictable; and the coverage of the written record by previous bibliographers much more uneven. Some of the surprises that turn up—the popularity of the topic in eighteenth-century Bulgaria, the fact that many of the authors were the progeny of Methodist ministers, the relevance of the topic to nuclear engineering — will probably engage readers as much as it does the compiler. The possibilities of redefining the scope, or spinning off part of the text as another study may need to be considered. Through revisions of earlier decisions on scope, style, content and arrangement, the final plan perfects itself, the main determinant of quality always being the ability of the list to describe the literature effectively for the benefit of readers.

The completion of the project needs to be seen in terms of two steps, of which the penultimate is the more spectacular and drastic. This step involves converting the 'working file' into the final copy by taking three actions: (1) arrange the entries, (2) number them, and (3) resolve, however painfully, that new materials will go into a second edition, the first supplement, appendix or wherever. This decision will usually be made when there are still loose ends floating about and before the index is prepared, an operation which in itself will turn up even more loose ends in need of decision or further research. This penultimate activity is best undertaken about 80 per cent of the way towards the deadline; 90 per cent at the very latest.

The last step for the compiler — short of delivering copy to a printer or publisher, proof-reading and awaiting the critical reception — is devoted to clean-up work of the file in its final form. Where the first stages of the project were concerned with getting into the project as efficiently and productively as possible, the final ones are concerned with getting out of it with as clean a conscience as possible. There will always be the search for evasive references; verification of spellings, dates or other details; decisions on matters delayed in the hope that time and later discoveries would provide guidance. At this point miscellaneous notations will help the compiler's memory. All of the last-minute detail takes more time and work than was planned; it is useful to add on 50 per cent to the original estimate for this activity. It is also worth remembering that the cost of nearing perfection approaches a point of diminishing returns: the differences between 99.9 and 99.99 per cent perfection is likely to cost as much as the difference between 1 and 50 per cent. While time itself may provide many of the needed answers, it also causes projects to become stale in the compiler's imagination: it is tempting to make the pronouncement that no bibliography of any size ought to be prepared in fewer than six weeks, or more than six years. In order to distinguish between perfection of style and perfection of coverage, experienced and sympathetic colleagues should be available to offer advice on when to compromise, when the temptation to cut corners calls for more work, total abandonment of an idea, or alternative practices of statement. But it is only the compiler who will know when the text is finally ready for God and for the malicious critic, as ready as he will ever be able to make it.

Computer applications have now become central to other sectors of the macrocosm of bibliographical organization, such as library cataloguing and continuing index programmes. If they would appear to be largely peripheral to this discussion, it is perhaps because of our concern mostly with means rather than ends. At the time of writing, the impact of the rapidly changing world of computers can perhaps be gathered under three topics: access to citations through online data bases (mentioned in the third section of this chapter); the role of the finite and perfected bibliographical list in relation to the open-ended bibliographical services, most of them online (discussed in Chapter VII); and the compiler's use of word-processing and similar equipment (mentioned in the second section of this chapter). The recent advent of the word-processor has obviously revolutionized the task of the indexer; and more refinements may be expected.

Clearly a major advantage of computer processing is the elimination of re-copying and duplicate processing, where errors so often creep in. Authors who have read page proofs—in which *theoretically* the only conceivable changes would result from instructions made on the earlier galley proofs—may protest the naïveté of such an altogether reasonable state of affairs. The high incidence of error in so many of the earliest computer-generated lists suggests that compilers were either lulled into a false sense of confidence, or too weak to argue with the powerful cost calculations of computer reprocessing activities. Ralph Shaw's visionary essays from the 1950s still make exciting reading,[16] for the reason that they make such good logical sense. The evidence to date suggests that the compiler can expect the computer to make for more logical and systematic procedures, but hardly to compensate for any lack of thoroughness. The compiler working through institutional auspices in particular should be prepared to be effective politically, rhetorically and logically in the cause of accuracy and detail.

WRITINGS ON THE USE OF COMPUTERS BY COMPILERS. Especially useful as of this writing should be the survey on 'Word Processing in Libraries', *Library Technology Reports* (American Library Association), vol. 16, no. 4 (July–August 1980), esp. 305–16, with a valuable glossary; and parts of Arthur H. Phillips, *Handbook of Computer-Aided Composition* (New York: Marcel Dekker, 1980). M. N. Lodder's supplement, 'The Application of Computers to Systematic Bibliography', on pp. 83–95 of the 1979 ed. of Robinson (1963) also deserves mention. In addition, Professor Victor Rosenberg of the University of Michigan has recently developed a software program based on the American National Standard for Bibliographic References. Such is the state of affairs, to my knowledge, as of early 1983; by the time this book appears, the picture will probably be quite different, and the literature addressed expressly to the needs of compilers may be much more extensive.

Beyond the purview of this study are co-operative bibliographical projects. Their number is legion, as must be the varieties of relationships between the several compilers: one strong on planning and the other on execution, one a dilatory perfectionist and the other a forceful expediter, several persons with special access to different library collections or other facilities and advantages, one the old and tired mentor with vast files and the other the young and energetic student in need of a reputation. The ultimate advantages of co-operation are broader and better definition of the project, more complete coverage, perhaps a more comprehensive or authoritative text, but never time-saving. It is probably not uncommon for two persons on a team to spend more time apiece than either would have spent alone doing the same work. Those projects in which the plan is obvious and incontrovertible at the outset are likely to be those best suited for co-operative efforts. In the final stages in particular, the ancient proof-reader's maxim should be recalled: 'four eyes are better than two'.

NOTES

1. Hardin Craig, 'How to be a Productive Scholar without any Time to Work', *American Scholar*, 35 (1965–66), pp. 126–8, may be worth posting on the bulletin board next to the compiler's desk.
2. Susan Warren Wilbur, in Appendix I to Llewelyn Jones, *How to Criticize Books* (New York: W. W. Norton, 1928), p. 183.
3. For a complementary perspective of this discussion specifically addressed to librarians but equally relevant to compilers in general, *see* Arthur Brown, 'The Text, the Bibliographer, and the Librarian', in *Otium et negotium: Studies in Onomatology and Library Science presented to Olof von Feilitzen* (Stockholm, 1973. Acta bibliothecae regiae stockholmiensis, 16.), pp. 23–31, the final passages in particular.
4. The context of this discussion is reflected in writings on the sociology of scholarship, notably in Robert K. Merton, 'The Perspectives of Insiders and Outsiders', *American Journal of Sociology*, 77 (1972), 9–47, and reprinted in his *The Sociology of Science* (Chicago: University of Chicago Press, 1973), pp. 99–136.
5. Beatrice Webb, 'The Art of Note-Taking', in *My Apprenticeship* (London: Longmans, Green, & Co., 1926), pp. 426–36.
6. For one special system, *see* E. J. Crossman and Cheryl D. Goodchild, 'A Way to Ease Preparation of Checklists and Bibliographies', *Scholarly Publishing*, 4 (1973), 245–9.
7. S. C. Bradford's 'law of scatter' is stated in his *Documentation* (2nd ed.; London: Crosby & Lockwood, 1953), p. 152: the aggregate number of articles in a given subject, apart from those produced by the first group of large producers, is proportional to the logarithm of the number of producers concerned, when those are arranged in order of decreasing population. The thrust of later discussions and derivative studies is summarized in M. Carl Drott, 'Bradford's Law: Theory, Empiricism, and Gaps Between', *Library Trends*, 30 (1981), 41–52.
8. Eugene Garfield, 'The Mystery of the Transposed Journal

Lists', in his *Essays of an Information Scientist*, vol. 1 (Philadelphia: ISI Press, 1977), p. 222.

9. Wilson, *Two Kinds of Power* (1968), pp. 58–9, 63n.

10. Gilbert J. Garraghan, *A Guide to Historical Method* (New York: Fordham University Press, 1957), pp. 139–40.

11. Hyatt (1980) discusses a part of this genre specifically, but also implicitly the whole genre. In proposing that 'writer's guides to periodical literature are hardy survivors of bibliography in a climate which threatens the extinction of their more delicate fellows' (p. 201), he is expressing a viewpoint with which I profoundly disagree; but he is also suggesting why they are assigned where they are in the sequence of operations that has been proposed here.

12. The quotation itself, epitomizing the valiant efforts of past leaders, is from Robert Bingham Downs' essay with this very title, 'No Book Should be out of Reach', *California Librarian*, 13 (December 1951), 77–80 and 110–11.

13. G. Thomas Tanselle, 'Book Jackets, Blurbs, and Bibliographers', *The Library*, 5th series, 26 (1971), 91–134.

14. Bourton (1956), p. 8.

15. F. W. Bateson, *The Scholar-Critic: An Introduction to Literary Research* (London: Routledge & Kegan Paul, 1979), p. 179.

16. Shaw's 1954 and 1964 essays, cited in the Bibliography, come particularly to mind.

CHAPTER VII

Presentation

THE TITLE

In naming the final list, the compiler must choose between a lively and engaging title that might seem too implicit, and a precise one that might seem too dull. While it is important to catch the eye, it is more important to use the title in a functional sense. Curiously, this turns out to be essentially negative—a means of sending away those who do not really need to use the list. It is rarely possible to specify all the major decisions of scope and function in titles that run fewer than three lines ('Books and . . ., excluding . . ., on the Subject of . . ., as defined by . . ., published between . . . and . . ., and found in . . ., for the Use of . . . in . . .: A Critically Annotated Bibliography'). One must select, ruthlessly and intelligently, with the reader rather than the literature in mind. It is sometimes possible to combine the implicit and the explicit by using a subtitle for the latter. A good example is Donald Wing's list of unlocated early English books entitled *A Gallery of Ghosts: Books Published between 1641–1700 not found in the Short-Title Catalogue*.[1] The implicit serves mostly to attract, the explicit to repel.

In using specific terms in the title and in the introduction, it is useful to recall several general distinctions usually made between the different kinds of lists. *Bibliography* ought to be reserved for detailed description of items that a compiler has examined as physical objects, while *catalogue* is appropriate when specific collections are concerned. A bibliography shows special respect for the needs of those studying texts, while a catalogue acknowledges a special commitment to rules for entry and description. The adjective 'short-title' implies just that: minimal titles, usually preceded by brief name forms, and followed by terse imprints and very few details. Bibliographies and catalogues may be designated as general or specialized; national, universal or international; historical, annotated, classified or chronological; descriptive, critical or analytical; retrospective or current. One also sees comprehensive or selective—both disturbing, in that each in its way is pretentious. The *list* is casual: *reading list* for non-specialist readers, *reference list* when brief consultation is intended, *check list* for the use of scholars, collectors or acquisitions librarians in checking their references and holdings, *finding list* when locations are specified or implied, *hand list* ambiguously for any, several or none of the above. *Inventory*, *repertory*, *manual* to the literature, even *report*, *guide* or *index* may be appropriate to specific cases.

Bibliography may originally have dealt with books, but today is loosely applied to all forms of library materials and potential library materials. The common extrapolations include such linguistic mongrels as *filmography*, and *rollography* for piano rolls. *Discography*, has outgrown its original connotation and covers sound recordings of all kinds—discs, wires, tapes, cassettes or cylinders. While the study of maps is today known as 'cartography', I know of no list of maps that goes by that name. Pictorial materials and other museum-like objects most commonly use the term *catalogue*. Sometimes the subject itself is named without any mention that the work is a list rather than a discussion of the subject.

THE INTRODUCTION AND OTHER FEATURES

There is a major problem with the compiler's introduction: most readers never notice it. They will turn to the entries; work out the sequence, possibly using the table of contents and the index if necessary; and extract what they need, laying the book aside when they fail. Time is too important. The introduction, which is in effect the compiler's annotation to his own work, will be useful to the minority of specialist readers for whom the work falls exactly in their area, as well as for reviewers, not to mention historians of scholarship and bibliometrics students. Such tidings should not deter the compiler in the least: a well-conceived introduction is important, even essential.

Its topics include a description of the plan of the work itself. Bates would require that these include comments on Wilson's five specifications: domain, scope, specificity, elements and organization. This could produce a somewhat literal-minded and pedestrian text; and other matters are no less worthwhile. In preparing this part of the text, the 'side file' of information (*see* Chapter VI, section on file organization) may be particularly useful. In discussing the scope, it is valuable to specify the kinds of materials that were excluded and the reasons for excluding them. Occasionally it is useful to explain to the reader how to use the list: what particular symbols mean, what to make of the statements, how and when to use the index, and why some things are as they are. The more idiosyncratic the plan, the more likely such matters will need to be explained.

Equally important is a very brief background on the topic, so as to make it clear that the compiler knows what he is doing. It is worth mentioning names, dates, events and attitudes for either the topic, its literature or both, possibly as part of the description of the list's scope. The compiler can most openly acknowledge biases at this point as a way of forestalling hostile critics. More important, this is the place to suggest dimensions to the presentation that the arrangement and indexes may not be able to bring out: single out particularly important works, describe relationships, call attention to lacunae and generally fill in the picture where necessary.

Finally, and usually at the end, come the acknowledgements. These may include books, institutions and persons; the text in question benefits from a mixture of lavishness, modesty, warm good spirits and absence of florid obsequiousness. Reading other authors' statements can be instructive. It is in a compiler's list of acknowledgements that many reviewers come up with some of their most important impressions of a project: where it was done, who provided advice, whose names are conspicuously absent and who provided support.

Among the acknowledgments can be included some of the features that would fit under Wilson's heading called 'domain'. It is useful for the compiler to identify sources, if not all of them at least the most productive and unusual. It is often appropriate to mention or suggest them in the introduction, in the discussion of the plan or of the topic, or even in the acknowledgments.

One reason for so conspicuous a statement of sources involves the protocols of reference. The copyright status of a bibliographical citation is far from unambiguous. Presumably it lies somewhere between that of recipes in a cookery book, which have little history in the courts but are probably hard to keep out of the public domain, and computer programs, which are now specifically protected. Since directories are protected, even unannotated lists would seem to be too. Bibliographic plagiarism, however, is a grey area in that it is likely to involve ideas and overall conception as much as specific formal statements. The stylistic formulation of the citations will presumably be reworked by compilers to fit the special needs of the list, so that, except when one copyrighted source can be shown to have provided a healthy proportion of the entries, the compiler is off the hook. Even so, acknowledgment of sources is ultimately evidence both of good work habits and good manners.

As for the 'negative successes' and failures, it would help the next compiler by citing them, although the precise place for such an acknowledgment is rarely convenient. Offering a long list of titles in the course of the introduction will tend to bog down the prose, besides reflecting more on the literal-mindedness than on the thoroughness of the compiler. Laudable as the objective may be, the realization is likely to be difficult to achieve with any graciousness.

In addition to the introduction, other condiments may be appropriate. For a classified list, a table of contents will almost certainly be mandatory. When appropriate a special directory of abbreviations, symbols or acronyms will be useful at the beginning. Other features, generally more gratuitous, belong at the end. A directory of addresses of issuing agencies of current publications

may be helpful. It is often valuable to have a special conspectus or
several of them at the end presenting the compiler's perspective on
the topic—a listing of pre-1701 titles arranged chronologically, of
Third World imprints arranged by country and city, or of other
classified items more useful standing in a systematic and tabular
form than scattered through the index. In such presentations, the
order of the elements will need to be re-arranged for optimum
scanning convenience, and not presented literally giving the
impression of a computer print-out for which the needed funds or
programming skills were not available. The index, at the very end,
should also be preceded by introductory comments as may be
necessary to explain policy decisions on name forms, terminology,
concepts and references.

WRITINGS ON WORKING WITH PUBLISHERS. Many of the style manuals listed
at the end of Chapter III (notably Butcher, MLA and Chicago) and many of
the general research guides cited in the bibliographical note 'Writings on
Research Procedures' early in Chapter VI (Mitchell, pp. 301ff. and 380ff.
being one of the best) discuss the preparation of manuscripts for
publication. The character of the genre of research guides is critically
explored by Naomi B. Pascal in the specific terms of 'Four More
Enchiridia', *Scholarly Publishing*, 10 (1979), 351–8. The appropriate
standards for the genre are suggested even more rigorously in Richard D.
Altick's 'This Will Never Do', *Review*, 1 (1979), 47–60, a review of
Margaret C. Patterson's *Literary Research Guide* (Detroit: Gale Research,
1980). Other general writings that discuss the relationship between the
scholarly creator and the specialist publisher include Judith Butcher,
Typescripts, Proofs, and Indexes (Cambridge: Cambridge University Press,
1980); Caroline D. Eckhardt, 'What Makes a Paper Publishable?' *French-
American Review*, vol. 3, no. 1 (1978–9), 1–5; John Farrar, 'Securing and
Selecting the Manuscript', in Chandler B. Grannis, *What Happens in Book
Publishing* (2nd ed. New York, London: Columbia University Press, 1967),
pp. 27–53; Robert S. Gill, *The Author Publisher Printer Complex* (3rd ed.
Baltimore: Williams & Wilkins, 1958); Savoie D. Lottinville, *The Rhetoric
of History* (Norman: University of Oklahoma Press, 1976), esp. chapter 10,
pp. 203–30 ('The Mote in the Publisher's Eye'), as well as pp. 140–6; and
Henry M. Silver, 'Putting it on Paper', *PMLA*, 56 (1950), 9–20. *The Oxford
Dictionary for Writers and Editors* (Oxford: Clarendon Press; New York:
Oxford University Press, 1981) is also valuable to know about. Finally, due
mention should be made of vol. 14, no. 4 (1980) of *Visible Language*, a
special issue devoted to the 'Dynamics of Writing'; for indeed one of the

cornerstones of this text is the belief that the compiler, like other writers, 'doesn't know what he is saying until he sees it on the page' (p. 382).

LAYOUT

The appearance of the text on the page is important for the readers who will be grateful for any efforts to save their time. With so many options in content the possibilities are vast. Despite the many past practices the specifics of visual mobility have not been widely studied. It might seem useful to wander through the bibliography section of a good library, picking books off the shelf and comparing the appearance of pages; unfortunately, experience suggests that this diversion is seldom productive. Robinson gives a brief anthology of examples which, while reduced in size, are almost as instructive and serve the requisite purpose with much less effort.

Since a bibliography is consulted strategically but very rarely read through, it follows that the more entries per page the better. As a medium to be scanned, the ideal bibliography might aspire to the appearance of a map, although the sensible restrictions of largeness in page size and smallness in type serve to remind us that the ideal may be quite a long way ahead. In type size anything above a 14-point face will seem pretentious and wasteful, anything below 8-point, hard to use. Because of the density of information, it is more important for the lines to be short, between 65 and 100 mm (approximately 2.5–4 inches) wide; in a normal book typeface, 65 mm would provide about 40 characters in 11-point or 43 in 10-point, whereas 100 mm would allow some 60 characters in 11-point or 65 in 10-point. When longer lines are used, internal information simply does not jump out at the reader: the reader's eye typically focuses on the middle of the column, veering to the left for the entry word near the top of the citation when scanning entries rather than whole pages. With both large pages and short lines desirable, a double- or even triple-column layout may be the reasonable if imperfect answer;[2] and with so many typically short statements, justified right margins are probably a needless luxury if not altogether inappropriate.

The manipulation of white space on the page can also be important. Individual entries should stand out and not run together; incomplete last lines may not differentiate enough for this purpose. A smaller amount of space between citation and annotation than between entries is also effective. On the other hand, vertical leading may actually slow down the eye, as the Spencer study observes. A hanging indention will also help to make the entry stand out. Underlinings are useful only as a signal to a printer to use italics; when left for the reader's eye, they call too much attention to what may need only to be contrasted. When italics are used, narrow columns and more luxurious vertical spacing seem appropriate. The effect of italics is both to set off a text and to break up the severity of statements that are essentially blunt and ungracious.

Indenting the annotation on the left is also useful; considering the many short statements involved, an inset at the right may be inappropriate in so far as it is detrimental to the suggestion of a right margin. The ideal overall effect, as Rollins notes, is likely to be one of steps, especially on the left margin. Unless the entry words are set in larger type to make them stand out, there is no point in beginning the title on a new line. Alternatively, in lists with typically long annotations, an inset citation and a flush-left annotation, in smaller type, may be effective. Some bibliographies use separate lines for different elements, in the citation and in the annotations, especially when the column is narrow; while such generosity is no doubt helpful, it may need to be sacrificed to use paper more efficiently.

A perennial design problem involves the entry number: its usefulness has been stressed, but where does one put it? The ideal place, at the left of the entry, both wastes space and may also detract from the first entry statements, which are typically the most important ones. Alternatives include the right margin at the end of the citation, or just below it when this statement runs too long; the left or right margin above the first line of the entry, or below the last line of the citation; the right margin in instances where the title will begin on a new line; or in a tucked-in corner of the citation (*see* Appendix C). There is no perfect solution, but guidance can often be found in other lists.

Although in recent years the trend has been to set everything in one type size and style, as the possibilities of computer setting come to be realized, a variety of sizes and style may become viable. It is nice when titles can be italicized; when the annotation can be one or two points smaller than the citation; when the entry and other important statements can be in bold face, or large and small caps. As appropriate type faces, Rollins liked several old style ones, as well as 'Scotch Roman' faces; other modern designers have put in good words for Baskerville and Times New Roman.

It may be thought visionary to place each bibliographical element in a separate column so as to facilitate scanning. However, examination of several bibliographies that use such a plan suggests that the advantages are not so great as imagined; our eyes are accustomed to picking out more than we realize, and more quickly. Yet to suggest that our conception of the appearance of a bibliographical citation will be the same one hundred years from now is undermined by the evidence of how citations have changed over the past century or two. So long as we oblige our readers with the respect and convenience of citations printed on paper, we can expect tastes to change. It is important for the compiler and designer to be as concerned with past solutions as with present possibilities of helping the reader. It is thus all the more unfortunate that this particular matter has previously been seldom discussed in print; such being the case, Appendix C must provide the best models.

WRITINGS ON THE LAYOUT OF BIBLIOGRAPHIES. The scanty literature begins auspiciously with Rollins (1923), but then jumps half a century to Spencer (1975), whose studies open up new prospects for confirming and criticizing aesthetic standards through psychological measurements. John Menapace, 'Some Approaches to Annotation', *Scholarly Publishing*, 1 (1970), 194–205, is a particularly useful and imaginative essay well worth the compiler's attention. Robinson (1963) also discusses layout (chapter 4 in the 1979 ed.) on pp. 79–81, as do Higgins (1941), pp. 36–40, and Robert L. Collison, *Indexes and Indexing* (4th revised ed. London: Ernest Benn; New York: John De Graff, 1972), particularly on pp. 84–97 ('Checking Layout Style: Collaboration with the Printer'). Stanley Rice, *Book Design* (London: R. R. Bowker, 1978), in vol. 2 (*Text Format Models*), pp. 95–98 and 202, discusses bibliographies specifically, with examples that are perhaps intentionally conservative so as to serve as the basis for appropriate adaptation. The general literature on book design includes, among the standard works, Ernest Reich, 'Designing the Physical Book', in Chandler B. Grannis, *What Happens in Book Publishing* (2nd ed. New York, London: Columbia University Press, 1967), pp. 80–91; Oliver Simon's classic *Introduction to Typography* (new ed. by David Bland. London: Faber & Faber, 1963); and John Trevitt, *Book Design* (Cambridge: Cambridge University Press, 1980). Vol. 15, no. 1 of *Visible Language* (1981) is a special issue devoted to 'The Spatial Arrangement of Text,' edited by James Hartley and Peter Burnhill.

When the text is to be used as printer's copy, all textual matter, including citations and annotations, should be submitted in the form that publishers and printers require—clean, neat double-spaced copy (everything must be double-spaced), with wide margins (top, bottom and both sides) and no word breaks at the ends of typed lines (someone else will only have to put the words back together or instruct the typesetter to insert the required hyphen), typed on to one side of a standard sized, opaque white paper (submit the original top copy, not a carbon or photocopy).

When the final copy is to be copied directly by camera, the compiler becomes the designer and typesetter. Before typing is commenced, the format should be agreed with the publisher if there is one at that stage, because the options are limitless: both citation and annotation on one and one-half spaces, the citation double-spaced and the annotation one and one-half, or the citation one and one-half and the annotation single-spaced; an extra line of space between the citation and the annotation, perhaps, and a greater amount of space between the entries; and different indentions for different elements of the entry. As the final typed copy is, in effect, the printer's reproduction proof, all corrections will have had to be made before final submission. Photographic reduction of standard typewritten faces up to 20 per cent may be considered to good effect, and typing on to larger than standard sized paper in two columns for reduction to a standard book size is possible. While the day when authors will be their own compositors of text is just around the corner and basically to be welcomed, its implications for the compiler are both drastic and promising: it will become an added responsibility to be more conversant with and sensitive to matters of book design, typography and graphic layout. Even today, one respected copy editor has been heard to nominate bibliographies as 'candidates for minimal editing . . . sometimes'. [3]

WRITINGS ON COPY PREPARATION. Among the writings that address the compiler's preparation of copy for the printer, Cowley (1939) has a good discussion in chapter 12 ('Editing the Completed Work', pp. 195–202). Other useful general discussions include William Bridgwater, 'Copy Editing', in Chandler B. Grannis, *What Happens in Book Publishing* (2nd ed. New York: Columbia University Press, 1967), pp. 54–79; Bruce Young, 'Manuscript Editing: Talent, Craft, and Sense of Order', *Scholarly Publishing*, 6 (1975), 229–33; and Karen Judd, *Copyediting: A Practical Guide* (Los Altos, Cal.: William Kaufmann, 1982); as well as other writings cited in the two bibliographical notes earlier in this chapter. In the one on proofreading below, the Lasky and McNaughton references are useful.

In proofreading bibliographical entries, the number of cryptic statements—one word or a few of them alone, many numbers, much punctuation—makes a two-person process (reader aloud plus copy-holder, or one person doing both with a tape recorder) mandatory. Such a noisy process is rarely possible in library reading rooms. In any event transcription errors seem most likely to enter when entries are first recorded—a matter that will plague the conscientious compiler, even at the final stage of proofreading. The two most common minor errors in the final lists are (1) errors in sequence, for instance involving simple alphabetization—a 'reading' of the final text (including indexes) is justified for this sole purpose; and (2) the failure of italicization, or underlining, to be carried over to a single word or short statement on a new line. Next to 'useful' it is well to remember that the kindest adjective to describe a bibliography is probably 'thorough'. [4] One distinguished scholar is said to have read everything three times, letter-by-letter, out loud, backwards. His vision is worth keeping in mind in what is a hopelessly tedious but absolutely necessary activity.

WRITINGS ON PROOFREADING. While I know of no writings devoted
specifically to the proofreading of bibliographies, compilers may find
ample guidance in the 656 (!) pages of Joseph Lasky, *Proofreading and Copy-
Preparation* (New York: Mentor Press, 1941), as well as Eleanor Harman,
'Hints on Proofreading', *Scholarly Publishing*, 6 (1975), 151–7; R. A. Hewitt,
Style for Print and Proof-Correcting (London: Blandford, 1957); Harry H.
McNaughton, *Proofreading and Copyediting* (New York: Hastings House,
1973); and Peggy Smith, *Proofreading Manual and Reference Guide* (Alexan-
dria, Va.: Editorial Experts, 1981), which on pp. 353–4 includes an
invaluable summary set of 'Proverbs for Proofreaders'.

PUBLICATION

Compilers enjoy seeing their names in print, reaping respect and
the trappings of academic credibility, even receiving some small
royalties and leaving to others the task of making copies and
circulating them. Many libraries, considering a changing function
for the circulation of materials and anticipating an improved loan
service in the near future, acquire almost anything that calls itself a
bibliography. It is understandable that publishers should spring up
in order to meet this demand. Similarly other organizations and
institutions see in bibliographies an opportunity to serve their
special audiences. Under these circumstances, compilers no longer
need to be annoyed at the indifference of those scholarly journals
that have regarded lists as beneath their intellectual dignity
(notwithstanding the lists of recent publications in so many of
them), or of those popular journals that have considered lists as too
dull for their readers (notwithstanding the occasional pieces
promoting 'books you might want to read').

The compiler may want to consider an alternative to formal
publication. Using today's inexpensive photocopying, it is easy to
circulate copies among the community of known specialists. In
some countries such costs can often be written off as personal tax
losses. Inexpensive copies can be distributed in lieu of Christmas
messages or for other festive occasions, or circulated in anticipation
of materials received in exchange. In the absence of an appropriate
publisher, the *samizdat* alternative is not unattractive.

Publication is an act of awesome finality, an irrevocable fall of the curtain: once in print, no errors can be corrected, no desirable refinements introduced, no opinions unfrozen. Publication also marks the beginning of the obsolescence of the list; for better or worse it creates monuments and induces rigor mortis. It imposes structure on the literature, which throughout subsequent history will itself be expanded and changing. The compiler's decision to embark on a bibliographical project, today as never before, reflects an act of faith that proposes not only that the effort is worthwhile in the first place, but also that the present time is auspicious to undertake it.

Small wonder then that scholars today should be strongly attracted to bibliographical records that are open-ended, expandable, and perfectable, where mistakes can be corrected quietly and new materials added with so little effort. Furthermore, today's facilities for online telecommunication make possible the integration of new entries from distant terminals and provide timely use for readers at other terminals. What then are the important functional differences between the 'culminated' or 'finalized' forms, which are the subject of this book, and the 'dynamic' and expandable bibliographical data bases? It is generally but not entirely correct, for instance, to equate the former with presentation on paper, and the latter with computers. Many major current bibliographical services are or were made available in printed form, their overriding drawback being the need to leaf through a frequently daunting array of bound back volumes and current unbound updatings—a task as inefficient as it is irritating. As a bibliography opts for a continuing instead of a finalized form, whether in a computer or on paper, it loses some things and gains others. Among the losses, the most basic is the predictable juxtaposition of entries, which on the one hand may be interrupted by an interpolated entry, and on the other may involve an important interpolated entry that the reader may miss finding out about. In any case, the bibliography becomes no longer a source to be read, but one merely to be consulted. How important this may be must be the compiler's decision—and challenge as well.

It should further be remembered that publication of a bibliography serves the very important purpose of promotion of the topic and its literature as well as for enhancing access. Computerized bibliographical activities came first to fields of scientific rather than humanistic information partly because of the greater affluence in the scientific fields, but also because of their preference for the timeliest rather than most venerable source. Equally important is the essential political neutrality of their writings. Objectivity is presumed. In contrast, writings in the humanistic and social fields, even when aspiring to scholarly objectivity, are also designed to influence human tastes and action, in which both rational and emotional considerations are mixed. One sector (what De Quincey called 'the literature of knowledge') calls for disinterested bibliographical access, to which the reader comes; the other (DeQuincey's 'literature of power') requires a pursuit and seduction of readers and in the process becomes part of the underlying political processes that define a civilization. Kepler as a scientist could announce his willingness to wait one hundred years for a reader, but for Disraeli and Durkheim, Dickens and Debussy, immediate exposure was essential.

In matters of quality the culminated list has built-in certain auspicious prospects. Finality requires the creator to suffer in the cause of having everything in place at the time of publication; there can be no loose ends, only full and correct entries or omissions. Everybody who gets in the vast group portrait must be in place, correctly exposed and smiling when the camera clicks. It is understandable then that authors should look hopefully to the less demanding and less punishing, open-ended forms of presentation. The fact remains that the anticipation of a final judgement day, and the resulting devastation of the human spirit, are likely to be essential to the quality of the work. The prospect of creating a timeless monument coupled with legends of erstwhile friends who open the first copy off the press at random and spot an error are some of the awesome forces that inspire a compiler's best labours. It is not that continuing lists do not offer the same or even better prospects for perfection of a text; rather, the finalized forms offer the mixture of vanity and terror that usually assures things getting done more effectively.

The updating of published bibliographies remains a very important matter, which Tanselle is among the few to have considered.[5] Two activities are involved: correcting old entries and fitting in new ones. In both the obstacle is one of timing — breakthroughs are just around the corner, so why not wait — and yet temporizing may be wrong. The mechanics of organizing published updating services, which Tanselle envisaged, are complicated by the infinite specialities of scholarly interest, and by the scholar's antipathy to looking for needles in haystacks. In time, with more continuing rather than culminated bibliographies, this problem would be solved; the present form would reflect the latest scholarship. Such a solution may seem simple, but the prospects may not be as good as we may hope. Most continuing programmes, being extensive in their activities, are highly cost-accountable; most bibliographical cost-accountability is based on so-called user studies; and most user studies now suggest (not entirely correctly, I think) that optimum use of materials comes within a short period after the first publication. In other words, things could happen, but they probably won't. In any event, Tanselle's proposal does need continued reconsideration, whether in terms of published copies on paper, continuing data bases, and not be overlooked, the most venerable, infuriating, reliable and perishable form: the walking human specialized encyclopaedia, accessible via telephone, postcard or in person.

The monument-conscious compiler in particular should be reminded that the most important bibliographies are those that come to be superseded. The scholarship almost always consists in expansion: there will be not only more entries, but also more elements in each citation. Failure along the way to correct errors creates particularly deserving targets, although the superseded lists themselves will continue as valuable source material for our significant and engaging studies in the history of learning.

EVALUATION

The final test of a bibliography will be performed by an unknown number of faceless readers, who extend across the face of the earth and into the indefinite future, and who will thank or curse the compiler, usually and unfortunately in silence. More immediate are those vocal users who will presume to offer considered judgements in the form of critical reviews or evaluative studies. By way of anticipating the thinking of both these groups, it is useful to summarize several of the most important statements of criteria on which bibliographical lists are to be judged.

John Shaw Billings specified five considerations: accuracy, completeness, absence of redundancy or repetition, form, and 'the most important . . ., that it should be such that a librarian or a bookseller can find the books called for with the least expenditure of time and trouble, and that the classification shall be such as will direct the inquirer most readily to the especial information which he seeks.' Schrero later preferred the four rubrics of accuracy, completeness, consistency and arrangement. A 1969 American Library Association committee moved back to Billings's five, with 'formal attractiveness' substituted for 'form'; 'originality' for 'absence of repetition'; and the other three statements much the same. Soon thereafter, another ALA committee prepared the statement reprinted in Appendix A, which provides our best detailed agenda for systematic critical appraisal of bibliographies in their own terms.

WRITINGS ON THE EVALUATION OF BIBLIOGRAPHIES. In addition to Billings (1883) and Schrero (1939), *see* the ALA's Subscription Books Committee *Manual* (Chicago: American Library Association, 1969), paragraph 101 ('Guidelines for Reviewing Bibliographic Reference Sources', pp. 31–4); also *see* William F. E. Morley and Flora E. Patterson, 'Criteria for the Evaluation of Enumerative Bibliographies' (draft manuscript, 1979, prepared for the Committee on Bibliographical Services for Canada), based largely on the 1971 ALA statement (Appendix A); and Harmon (1981), chapter 12 ('Evaluating Bibliographies', pp. 142–7).

Simon (1973) is among the first to propose a special study of the analysis of bibliographies. The study of footnoting and other internal reference practices, as surveyed in Linda C. Smith, 'Citation Analysis', *Library Trends*, 30 (1981), 83–106, is essentially a different field of inquiry, although there is an obviously large grey area between those prose texts that mention other prose texts, and bibliographical records that serve exclusively as a means of conveying citations. Such being the case, the impact of citation analysis on the analytical study of bibliographies will always be implicit, if not yet usefully explicit. Commentators on bibliographies, of course — whether in reviews, essays, or annotations — have long recognized the usefulness of side-by-side comparisons of related lists, and often called on statistical data in presenting their conclusions. Among many examples that might be cited, a rather good one is D. Kathryn Weintraub, 'Three British Bibliographic Services: A Study of Duplication', *Library Quarterly*, 32 (1962), 199–207. The literature devoted to the perceptive criticism and evaluation of individual bibliographies is obviously huge; and the daunting prospect is that one of the most valuable successors to this book would involve some kind of bibliographical survey of this material.

As a genre, bibliographies should continue to be useful in so far as their delimited objectives are addressed. Through citation and annotation practices that are thoughtfully tailored to be lean, efficient, and strategically focused, and through organizational plans and visual arrangements designed to point up unsuspected relationships, they can stay close to their intended audience. As autonomous entrepreneurial projects, they attract compilers and sponsors willing to commit their efforts to the special cause of the particular topic being covered, and willing eventually to be evaluated in matters of expertise by the rigorous community of specialists. [6]

Typically small in size and fixed in time, they further serve to question some of our prevalent assumptions about efficiency in size. They argue collectively that our bibliographical macrocosm needs both the 'tight', large-scale, bureaucratic forms, and the 'loose', intimate, and unpredictable forms that they represent. As such, bibliographies serve to work against monopolies of knowledge in so far as they may help to re-structure them. They improve the macrocosm both by contributing to its records, and also by offering prospects for its analysis and re-definition. Bibliographies will be around, in any event, as long as they are needed. That being the case, this book may be useful in calling attention to their particular merits and appropriate practices.

NOTES

1. New York: Modern Language Association, Index Committee, 1967.
2. Notwithstanding Rollins' respected reservations about double

columns, as enunciated in 'Gilding the Lily: In the Designing of Books There's No Sin like Complacency', in E. S. Miers and R. Ellis, *Bookmaking and Kindred Amenities* (New Brunswick: Rutgers University Press, 1942), p. 29.

3. Naomi B. Pascal, 'How Much Editing is Enough', *Scholarly Publishing*, 13 (1982), 267.

4. Appropriate analogies may be found in John B. Bennett, 'Books by their Covers: The Importance of Style', *Society of Technical Writers and Publishers Review*, vol. 9, no. 2 (1962), 20. The point cannot be better stated for librarians and bibliographers than in Richard D. Altick, *Librarianship and the Pursuit of Truth* (New Brunswick: Rutgers University, Graduate School of Library Service, 1974; Richard H. Shoemaker Lecture for 1972).

5. G. Thomas Tanselle, 'A Proposal for Recording Additions to Bibliographies', *Papers of the Bibliographical Society of America*, 62 (1968), 227–36.

6. Readers may recognize phrases and ideas here that reflect on the 'basic traits' identified in Thomas J. Peters and Robert H. Waterman, Jr, *In Search of Excellence: Lessons from America's Best-Run Companies* (New York: Harper & Row, 1982) —admittedly an unlikely model for this discussion, but also something of a timely coincidence.

APPENDIX A

Criteria for
Evaluating a Bibliography

A statement prepared by the Bibliography Committee of the Reference Services Division, American Library Association, and published in *RQ*, 11 (1972), 359–60. Some of the provisions have been refined in a later statement, as published in *RQ*, 22 (1982), 31–2; but the revised statement serves a somewhat different purpose, as reflected in the new title, 'Guidelines for the Preparation of a Bibliography'. The original statement is reproduced here by permission of the American Library Association.

I. Subject matter
    A. Subject matter should be clearly defined in the title or in some preliminary statement.
    B. The subject should be significant—not necessarily large, it may be quite limited—but there should be some reason for compiling a bibliography on it.
    C. It should fit into the general scheme of bibliography (if there is one). It should not duplicate an existing bibliography at the same level.
    D. If there are similar bibliographies, a new one should make a unique contribution of sufficient importance to justify whatever repetition is involved.

II. Scope within subject matter
    A. Bibliography may aim at completeness—all pertinent

literature within the subject matter framework, or it
may have further limitations:

1. Subjective—value judgments of the compiler, i.e.,
   Best Books
2. Objective limitations such as:
   a. Period
   b. Language
   c. Country or other geographic area
   d. Form: Literary form or form of publication
   e. Level of treatment: Popular, technical, etc.
   f. Bibliographical units (i.e., units cited as an entity
      in a bibliography such as a book, chapter of a
      book, journal article, report, manuscript, phono-
      record, music score, film, or chart) from one or
      more sources as holdings of a library, or references
      on rural electrification in the Bibliography of
      Agriculture.

III. Methodology
   A. It is helpful to anyone evaluating a bibliography if the
      principal sources consulted are given and some infor-
      mation is provided on the method of compilation.
      When this has been done, the evaluator can make the
      following tests:
      1. Have all important pertinent sources been consulted?
      2. Has the method been such that important materials
         might well have been missed?
      If this information is not given, methodology can only
      be deduced from the completeness of the resulting
      bibliography.
   B. So far as possible, the compiler should work with the
      bibliographical units rather than exclusively with bib-
      liographies. Units he has not personally examined
      should be marked to indicate this.

IV. Organization
   A. Should be suitable for the subject.
   B. Should make it possible to use the bibliography from at
      least one approach without consulting the index.

C. Classification for a classified subject bibliography should be logical and easy for intended users to understand.

D. Evaluation of Indexes
   1. Indexes should be complete.
   2. Indexes should be of a suitable level of analysis.
   3. Terminology should be suitable for subject and intended users.
   4. Cross references should be adequate.

E. Cumulation: Cumulation of serial bibliographies of the indexes thereof is highly desirable.

F. Other aids to use
   1. Preface, introduction or some preliminary statement of scope and purpose.
   2. If abbreviations are used they should be intelligible or a key should be provided.
   3. A table of contents should be provided unless the arrangement is very simple.
   4. The location of copies of bibliographical units is helpful.

V. Annotations—abstracts
   A. These may be at one of three levels:
      1. Informative notes used chiefly when title is not clear: These should show reason for inclusion of questionable titles.
      2. Abstracts: Should give enough of the contents to enable the user to decide accurately whether he wants to read the original, or in some cases, to enable him to dispense with such readings.
      3. Critical evaluations: These should be discriminating and should be written by someone competent to do the job.
   B. In each case they should be succinct and on a level suitable for the use intended.

VI. Bibliographic form
   A. There should be sufficient information to identify the bibliographic unit easily for the purpose of the intended user.

    B. The form should be the simplest consistent with A.

    C. The form should be followed consistently.

VII. Timeliness

    A. Current bibliographies should be issued promptly with a minimum of time lag between the publication of the bibliographical units listed and the publication of the bibliography.

    B. Retrospective bibliographies, except in cases in which by limitation of subject matter or scope recent bibliographical units are not included (e.g., Contemporary writings on Napoleon) should keep the time lag between closing the bibliography and its publication to a minimum.

VIII. Accuracy

    A. Citations should be correct and free from typographical errors.

    B. Information provided in annotations, etc. should be correct and annotations should be correct in spelling, sentence structure.

IX. Evaluation of format

    A. Should be legible.

    B. Sturdiness and permanence should be adapted to anticipated use.

    C. Insofar as possible, format should be designed to keep the price of the bibliography within the means of the potential users, or a large number of them, without sacrificing legibility or other features really important for ease of use.

APPENDIX B

Bibliographies as Evidence of Intellectual Eminence

The American Library Association statement in Appendix A is basically concerned with the reference usefulness of bibliographies. The question of intellectual eminence and achievement as reflected in a bibliography, while addressed by the same evidence, is somewhat different. It arises as bibliographies may need to be evaluated alongside and in comparison with books, essays, reviews and other prose presentations. The common instances involve decisions to be made in consideration of honours or special recognition for a compilation (for instance, book awards for bibliographies) or for a compiler (academic promotion or tenure on the basis of bibliographies). The text of this book suggests the following appropriate criteria:

1. The scope should be convincingly defined so as to establish the compiler as a recognized member of the intended audience. It should be implemented so as to include (a) everything that the community of experts in the subject will know about; (b) ideally, a few things that its individual members may not know about; and (c) all of what an aspiring expert ought to know about.

2. The citation style must be easy to grasp by, convincing to, and consistent with the needs of the intended readers.

3. The annotations, if present, should give evidence that the

compiler has brought out important details of particular entries that readers should but may not know about.

4. The list should be arranged, and complemented by indexes and other features, so as to provide access for all the legitimate inquiries of the specialized readers who are being addressed. The organization should further be commended insofar as it brings out unusual interrelationships of potential interest to the readers.

5. A list that is handsome and well designed is a credit to the compiler; it reflects on the respect of the publisher, as it will also promote the respect of the readers who use it.

6. A strong introductory essay, as it explicitly addresses the question of why the list is important and how it is to be used, also implicitly addresses the question of the intellectual achievement.

APPENDIX C

Awards to Bibliographies for Graphic Excellence

The bibliographies listed below have been honoured for their graphic design. Volumes of prose with extended and significant bibliographies are included; excluded are a number of catalogues of paintings, artifacts and other museum objects which, however closely analogous to books in their descriptive statements, are typically not found in library collections. The entries are arranged by date of publication.

UNITED STATES

Bibliographies listed in the American Institute of Graphic Arts catalogues of *Fifty Books of the Year* (New York, 1923–75), and later in the larger selections shown and listed in the *AIGA Book Show* series. The latest published catalogue of a Book Show, for 1979, appears in *Graphic Design USA, 1: The Annual of the AIGA*, written by C. Ray Smith (New York: Watson-Guptill Publications, 1980), pp. 367–425.

A History of Printing in Colonial Maryland. By Lawrence C. Wroth. Baltimore: Typothetae of Baltimore, 1922.   (1)

Catalogue of the John Carter Brown Library, Volume II, Part II: 1634–1658. Providence: Published by the Library; Boston: Merrymount Press, 1923.   (2)

The Richard C. Jenkinson Collection of Books, Chosen to Show the Work of the Best Printers. Newark, N.J.: The Public Library, 1925. (3)

Bruce Rogers, Designer of Books. By Frederic Warde, with a List of the Books printed under Mr Rogers's Supervision. Cambridge: Harvard University Press, 1926. (4)

Bibliography of the Works of Rudyard Kipling. By Flora V. Livingston. New York: Edgar H. Wells & Co, 1927. (5)

Thomas Hardy, 1840–1928: Catalogue of a Memorial Exhibition of First Editions, Autograph Letters and Manuscripts. Prepared by Richard L. Purdy. New Haven: Yale University Press, 1928. (6)

American First Editions: Bibliographic Check Lists of the Works of One Hundred and Five American Authors. Edited by Merle Johnson. New York: R. R. Bowker Co, 1929. (7)

Mason Locke Weems: His Works and Ways in Three Volumes. A Bibliography left unfinished by Paul Leicester Ford, edited by Emily Ellsworth Ford Skeel. Norwood, Mass.: Plimpton Press, 1929. (8)

Private Presses and their Books. By Will Ransom. New York: R. R. Bowker Co., 1929 (9)

A Bibliography of the Writings of Henry James. By LeRoy Phillips. New York: Coward-McCann, Inc., 1930. (10)

A Catalogue of the Altschul Collection of George Meredith in the Yale University Library. Compiled by Bertha Coolidge, with an Introduction by Chauncey Brewster Tinker. Boston: D. B. Updike, Merrymount Press, 1931. (11)

Descriptive Catalogue of Japanese and Chinese Illustrated Books in the Ryerson Library of the Art Institute of Chicago. By Kenji

Toda. Chicago: Lakeside Press, R. R. Donnelley & Sons, 1931.
(12)

American First Editions: Bibliographic Check Lists of the Works of 146 American Authors. Revised and Enlarged by Merle Johnson. New York: R. R. Bowker Co., 1932. (13)

A Bibliography of the Works of Robinson Jeffers. By S. S. Alberts. New York: Random House, 1933. (14)

The Catalogue of the Collection of Joseph T. Tower, Jr, Class of 1921, in the Institute of Geographic Exploration, Harvard University. Boston: Merrymount Press, D. B. Updike, 1933.
(15)

A Check List of Fifteenth Century Books in the Newberry Library and in other Libraries of Chicago. Compiled by Pierce Butler. Chicago: Newberry Library, 1933. (16)

Early American Children's Books. By A. S. W. Rosenbach, with Bibliographical Descriptions of the Books in his Private Collection; Foreword by A. Edward Newton. Portland, Maine: Southworth Press, 1933. (17)

Fifty Books about Bookmaking. Compiled with an Introduction by Hellmut Lehmann-Haupt. New York: Columbia University Press, 1933. (18)

Bibliography of the Writings of Edgar A. Poe. By John W. Robertson. San Francisco: Russian Hill Private Press, Edwin & Robert Grabhorn, 1934. (19)

Notes on the Merrymount Press and its Work. By Daniel Berkeley Updike; with a Bibliographical List of Books printed at the Press, 1893–1933, by Julian Pearce Smith; with Views of the Press at Various Periods, Specimens of Types alluded to . . . . Cambridge: Harvard University Press, 1934. (20)

A Bibliography of the Works of Mark Twain, Samuel Langhorne Clemens: A List of the First Editions in Book Form and of First Printings in Periodicals and Occasional Publications of his Varied Literary Activities. Revised and enlarged by Merle Johnson. New York: Harper and Brothers, 1935.   (21)

Samuel Richardson: A Bibliographical Record of his Literary Career. With Historical Notes by William Merritt Sale, Jr. New Haven: Yale University Press, 1936.   (22)

A Bibliography of Material Relating to Private Presses. By Irvin Haas, with an Introduction by Will Ransom. Chicago: The Black Cat Press, 1937.   (23)

Henry R. Wagner's The Plains and the Rockies: A Bibliography of Original Narratives of Travel and Adventure, 1800–1865. Revised and expanded by Charles L. Camp. San Francisco: Grabhorn Press, 1937.   (24)

Tobacco: Its History illustrated by the Books, Manuscripts and Engravings in the Library of George Arents, Jr. Together with an Introductory Essay, a Glossary, and Bibliographic Notes by Jerome E. Brooks. Volume One: 1507–1615. New York: Rosenbach Company, 1937.   (25)

A Catalogue of the Books of John Quincy Adams deposited in the Boston Athenaeum, with Notes on Books, Adams Seals and Book-plates. By Henry Adams, with an Introduction by Worthington Chauncey Ford. Boston: Printed for the Athenaeum, 1938.   (26)

Eighteenth Century North Carolina Imprints, 1749–1800. By Douglas C. McMurtrie. Chapel Hill: University of North Carolina Press, 1938.   (27)

Quintus Horatius Flaccus: Editions in the United States and Canada as they appear in the Union Catalog of the Library of Congress. Oakland, California: Mills College, 1938.   (28)

T. E. Lawrence: A Bibliography. By Elizabeth W. Duval. New York: Arrow Editions, 1938. (29)

Goethe's Works, with the Exception of Faust: A Catalogue. Compiled by Members of the Yale University Library Staff; Edited, arranged and supplied with Literary Notes, and Preceded by an Introduction and a Biographical Sketch of William A. Speck by Carl Frederick Schreiber. New Haven: Yale University Press, 1940. (30)

Maps of Connecticut before the Year 1800: A Descriptive List. By Edmund Thompson. Windham, Conn.: Hawthorn House, 1940. (31)

Bibliography of the Grabhorn Press, 1915–1940. By Elinor Raas Heller & David Magee. San Francisco: Grabhorn Press, 1941. (32)

A Bibliography of the Strawberry Hill Press, with a Record of the Prices at which Copies have been sold, together with a Bibliography and Census of the Detached Pieces. By A. T. Hazen and J. P. Kirby. New Haven: Yale University Press, 1942. (33)

The Fortsas Bibliohoax. By Walter Klinefelter, with a Reprint of the Fortsas Catalogue and Bibliographical Notes and Comment by Weber DeVore, New York: Press of the Woolly Whale, 1942. (34)

Guide to the Manuscript Collections in the William L. Clements Library. Compiled by Howard H. Peckham. Ann Arbor: University of Michigan Press, 1942. (35)

The Maps of the California Gold Region, 1848–1857: A Bibliocartography of an Important Decade. By Carl I. Wheat. San Francisco: Grabhorn Press, 1942. (36)

A Bio-Bibliography of Andreas Vesalius. By Harvey Cushing. New York: Schuman, 1943. (37)

Painting and Sculpture in the Museum of Modern Art. Edited by
Alfred H. Barr, Jr. New York: Museum of Modern Art, 1943.
                                                              (38)

Types and Bookmaking, containing Notes on the Books printed at
the Southworth-Anthoensen Press by Fred Anthoensen. And a
Bibliographical Catalogue, by Ruth A. Chaplin. With Specimens of its Work, Types, Borders .... Portland, Maine:
Southworth-Anthoensen Press, 1943.   (39)

A Bibliography of James Whitcomb Riley. By Anthony J. Russo
and Dorothy R. Russo. Indianapolis: Indiana Historical Society,
1944.   (40)

Renaissance Guides to Books: An Inventory and Some Conclusions. By Archer Taylor. Berkeley, Los Angeles: University
of California Press, 1945.   (41)

The Little Magazine: A History and a Bibliography. By Frederick
J. Hoffman, Charles Allen, Carolyn F. Ulrich. Princeton:
Princeton University Press, 1946.   (42)

A Bibliography of Oliver Wendell Holmes. By Thomas Franklin
Currier, Edited by Eleanor M. Tilton for the Bibliographical
Society of America. New York: University Press,
1953.   (43)

Italian Manuscripts in the Pierpont Morgan Library: Descriptive
Survey of the Principal Italian Illuminated Manuscripts of the
Sixth to Sixteenth Centuries, with a Selection of Important
Letters and Documents. Catalogue compiled by Meta Harrsen
and George K. Boyce, with an Introduction by Bernard
Berenson. New York: Pierpont Morgan Library, 1953.   (44)

Bibliography of American Literature, Volume One: Henry
Adams to Donn Byrne. Compiled by Jacob Blanck for the
Bibliographical Society of America. New Haven: Yale Uni-
versity Press, 1955.   (45)

Carl Van Vechten: A Bibliography. Compiled by Klaus W. Jonas, with a Preamble by Grace Zaring Stone. New York: Alfred A. Knopf, 1955. (46)

Central European Manuscripts in the Pierpont Morgan Library. Compiled by Meta Harrsen. New York: Pierpont Morgan Library, 1958. (47)

Tobacco: A Catalogue of the Books, Manuscripts and Engravings acquired since 1942 in the Arents Tobacco Collection. Part I: 1507–1571. Compiled by Sarah Augusta Dickson. New York: New York Public Library, 1958. (48)

Catalogue of Botanical Books in the Collection of Rachel McMasters Miller Hunt: Volume II, part II: Printed Books, 1701–1800. Compiled by Allan Stevenson. Pittsburgh: Hunt Botanical Library, 1961. (49)

The Ward Ritchie Press, and Anderson, Ritchie and Simon. By Ward Ritchie. Los Angeles: The Ward Ritchie Press, 1961. (50)

Huntia: A Yearbook of Botanical and Horticultural Bibliography. George H. M. Lawrence, ed. Pittsburgh: Hunt Botanical Library, Carnegie Institute of Technology [1964]. (51)

French 16th-Century Books, Volumes I and II. Compiled by Ruth Mortimer under the Supervision of Philip Hofer and William A. Jackson. Cambridge: Belknap Press of Harvard University Press, 1965. (52)

The Spiral Press through Four Decades. Introduction by Joseph Blumenthal. New York: Pierpont Morgan Library, 1966. (53)

The Arts of the French Book, 1900–1965: Illustrated Books of the School of Paris. By Eleanor M. Garvey and Peter A. Wick, Dallas: Southern Methodist University Press, for the Friends of the Dallas Public Library, 1967. (54)

The White House Library: A Short Title List. Compiled by James
T. Babb. Washington: White House Historical Association,
1967. (55)

Oregon Imprints, 1845–1870. By George N. Belknap. Eugene:
University of Oregon Books, 1968. (56)

The Fifty Books: Honoring Volumes published in 1968 and
Selected for Exhibition in 1969. New York: American Institute
of Graphic Arts, 1969. (57)

The Books of WAD: A Bibliography of the Books designed by
W. A. Dwiggins. Compiled by Dwight Agner, with a
Foreword by Alexander Lawson. Baton Rouge: The Press of the
Nightowl, 1974. (58)

Major Acquisitions of the Pierpont Morgan Library, 1924–1974.
By Charles Ryskamp, Herbert Cahoon, Felice Stamfle, Paul
Needham, William Voelkle. New York: Pierpont Morgan
Library, 1974. (59)

The Prints of Rockwell Kent: A Catalogue Raisonné. By Dan
Burne Jones. Chicago: University of Chicago Press, 1975.
(60)

The Pennsylvania German Fraktur of the Free Library of Philadelphia: An Illustrated Catalogue. Compiled by Frederick S.
Weiser and Howell J. Heaney. Volume One. Brenigsville: The
Pennsylvania German Society and the Free Library of Philadelphia, 1976. (61)

Reader, Lover of Books, Lover of Heaven: A Catalogue based on
an Exhibition of the Book Arts in Ontario, Compiled by David
B. Kotin, with a Checklist of Ontario Private Presses by
Marilyn Rueter and an Introduction by Douglas Lochhead.
Willowdale: North York Public Library, 1978. (62)

The Rowfant Manuscripts. By H. Jack Lang, with an Introduction

by Herman W. Liebert. Cleveland: The Rowfant Club, 1979.
(63)

Twelve Centuries of Bookbindings, 400–1600. By Paul Needham.
New York: Pierpoint Morgan Library; London: Oxford University Press, 1979.   (64)

In addition, the following bibliography (along with others cited
above) is honoured in the catalogue on *Les artes del libro en los estados
unidos* (Nueva York: Instituto Norteamericano de artes graficos,
1942):

A Bibliography of the Village Press, 1903–1938. By Melbert B.
Cary, Jr; Including an Account of the Genesis of the Press by
Frederic W. Goudy and a Portion of the 1903 Diary of Will
Ransom, Co-Founder. New York: Press of the Woolly Whale,
1938.   (65)

WEST GERMANY

Bibliographies honoured by the Stiftung Buchkunst of the
Börsenverein des Deutschen Buchhandels, as listed in the annual
catalogues entitled *Die schönsten Bücher des Jahres*, 1952–5; *Die
schönsten deutschen Bücher des Jahres*, 1956–69; and *Die fünfzig
Bücher*, 1970 forwards.

Bibliographie deutscher Schreibmeisterbücher von Neudörffer bis
1800. Von Werner Doede. Hamburg: Dr Ernst Hauswedell,
1958.   (66)

Fifty Mediaeval and Renaissance Manuscripts (Catalogue 88).
New York: H. P. Kraus, 1958.   (67)

Stefan George und sein Kreis: Eine Bibliographie. Von Georg
Peter Landmann. Hamburg: Dr Ernst Hauswedell, 1960. (68)

Die Walbaum Schriften und ihre Vorläufer: Eine Schriftstudie.

Von Gustav Bohadti. Berlin: H. Berthold AG Messinglinien-
fabrik und Schriftgiesserei, 1960.   (69)

Twenty-Five Manuscripts (Catalogue 95). New York: H. P.
Kraus, 1961.   (70)

Thirty-Five Manuscripts: Catalogue 100. New York: H. P. Kraus,
1962.   (71)

Deutsche Buchkunst 1890–1960, Band II: Abbildungen und
Bibliographie. Hamburg: Maximilian-Gesellschaft, 1963. (72)

Die Handschriften der Württembergischen Landesbibliothek
Stuttgart, II. . . ., 3: Codices iuridici et politici; Patres.
Beschrieben von Johanne Autenrieth. Wiesbaden: Otto Har-
rassowitz, 1963.   (73)

Katalog der Rilke-Sammlung Richard von Mises. Herausgegeben
von Paul Obermüller und Herbert Steiner, unter Mitarbeit von
Ernst Zinn. Frankfurt-am-Main: Insel Verlag, 1966.   (74)

Bibliographie der Hamburger Drucke des 16. Jahrhunderts. Von
Werner Kayser und Claus Dehn. Mitteilungen aus der Hambur-
ger Staats- und Universitätsbibliothek, Band 6. Hamburg: Dr
Ernst Hauswedell, 1968.   (75)

Werkstatt Rixdorfer Drucke: Oeuvre Verzeichnis. Herausgegeben von Heinz Ohff. Hamburg: Merlin Verlag, 1970. (76)

Frankfurter Buchmesse, Frankfurt Book Fair, Foire du livre de
Francfort, 18.9–3.10.1972: Katalog. Frankfurt-am-Main: Börsenvereins des Deutschen Buchhandels, 1972.   (77)

Books about Books: An International Exhibition on the Occasion
of the Interntational Book Year 1972. Frankfurt-am-Main:
Börsenvereins des Deutschen Buchhandels, 1972.   (78)

Kaufrufe und Strassenhändler, Cries and Itinerant Trades: Eine

Bibliographie, A Bibliography. Karen F. Beall. Hamburg: Dr Ernst Hauswedell, 1975. (79)

Supellex epistolica Uffenbachii et Wolfiorum: Katalog der Uffenbach-Wolfschen Briefsammlung. Herausgegeben und bearbeitet von Dr Nilüfer Krüger. Hamburg: Dr Ernst Hauswedell, 1978. (80)

Mittelalterliche Bibliothekskataloge Deutschlands und der Schweiz. Herausgegeben von der Bayerische Akademie der Wissenschaft in München. Iv. Band, 2. Teil: Bistum Freising, bearbeitet von Günter Glauche; Bistum Würzburg, bearbeitet von Hermann Knaus, mit Beiträgen von Bernhard Bischoff und Wilhelm Stoll. München: C. H. Beck, 1979. (81)

Der Frühdrucke in deutschen Südwesten, 1473–1500, Band 1: Ulm. Auustellung und Katalog: Peter Amelung. Stuttgart: Württenbergische Landesbibliothek, 1979. (82)

OTHER NATIONS

Awards in other countries are not listed in a single source so as to allow for any definitive record of the bibliographies that have been honoured. Austrian titles (awarded since 1953) often appear in the *Anzeiger des Österreichischen Buchhandels*; Danish titles (since 1934) in the *Årets bestebøger* of the Forening for Boghaandvaerk. Those from Sweden (since 1933), Switzerland (since 1944), Hungary (since 1957), Poland (since 1958) and Rumania (since 1962) are now usually exhibited at the Frankfurt Book Fair, and often described in the *Börsenblatt für Deutschen Buchhändler*.

BIBLIOGRAPHY

Major Writings on the Compiling of Bibliographies 1883–1983

An asterisk (*) indicates a copy not examined.

1. Billings, John Shaw. 'Medical Bibliography'. *Transactions of the Medical and Chirurgical Faculty of Maryland*, 1883, pp. 58–80. Reprinted in *Selected Papers of John Shaw Billings*, compiled by Frank Bradway Rogers (n.p.: Medical Library Association, 1965), pp. 149–69. Observations by the founding father of American medical bibliography and librarianship. The doctor ultimately must evaluate the bibliographical record in the course of asking how it addresses his particular needs.

2. Grand, Ernest D. 'Bibliographie', in *La grande encyclopèdie*, vol. 6 (Paris: Lamirault, 1888), pp. 598–682. A monumental survey of all aspects of bibliography, addressing matters of citation in section 3 ('Règles bibliographiques', pp. 613–33), with special concern for cataloguing practices for early books. The bibliographical references, throughout the text and on pp. 640–1 especially, offer a valuable survey of the earlier literature.

3. Madan, Falconer. 'On Method in Bibliography'. *Transactions of the Bibliographical Society*, 1 (1893), 91–102. Having indent-

ified four weaknesses in most bibliographical practice — inaccuracy and scantiness of information, ultra-scientific accuracy and superfluity of information, artificiality of conventions, and want of perspective — the notable Bodleian librarian sets forth his method for citation, and appends an anthology for Oxford books.

4. Campbell, Frank. *The Theory of National and International Bibliography*. London: Library Bureau, 1896. Visionary essays on the cause of universal bibliographic control, mostly reprinted from other sources. Many of the pieces include valuable points on the theory and practice of compilation, among them for instance one 'On the Evils of Short-Title Catalogues' (pp. 279–91).

5. Ferguson, John. *Some Aspects of Bibliography*. Edinburgh: George P. Johnston, 1900. Reprinted, Forest Hills, N.Y.: Battery Park Book Co., 1978. An early bibliographer of the history of chemistry here expands his 1899 presidential address for the Edinburgh Bibliographical Society, concerned with the kinds and uses of lists.

6. Cole, George Watson. 'Compiling a Bibliography'. *Library Journal*, 26 (1901), 791–5, 859–63. Advice addressed mostly to the then numerous compilers of local and county bibliographies, but with well-considered suggestions for compilers in general.

7. Brown, James Duff. 'Practical Bibliography'. *The Library*, 4 (1903), 144–51, with a response by A. W. Pollard, pp. 151–62. A pre-eminent English public librarian lashes out at the bibliographer's concern for the physical item, and holds up an ideal of studying what books are 'all *about*'. In turn, Pollard of the British Museum regrets Brown's intemperate narrow-mindedness and offers an understated defense of the cause of scholarly study of the printed book.

8. Brown, James Duff. *A Manual of Practical Bibliography*.

London: George Routledge & Sons, 1906. Brown sets forth his method, which is intended to serve the needs both of compilers and of library cataloguers.

9. Savage, Ernest A. *Manual of Descriptive Annotation for Library Catalogues.* London: Library Supply Co., 1906. Another scholarly English public librarian shows how to prepare descriptive notes on library catalogue cards, along the way establishing detailed practices still valuable today.

10. Pollard, A. W. 'The Arrangement of Bibliographies'. *The Library*, n.s., 10 (1909), 168–87. A landmark essay discussing the characteristics of alphabetical, chronological, and systematic arrangement of entries.

11. Pollard, A. W. 'Bibliography and Bibliology', in *Encyclopaedia Britannica*, 11th ed. (Cambridge: University Press, 1910), vol. 3, pp. 908–11. Also in the 14th ed. (Chicago: Encyclopaedia Britannica, 1949), vol. 3, pp. 539–41. The brief passage on 'Enumeration and Arrangement' is particularly well conceived.

12. Josephson, Aksel G. S. 'Efficiency and Bibliographical Research'. *Papers of the Bibliographical Society of America*, 7 (1912–13), 7–21. Bibliographical research is defined here as the organized pursuit of 'desired information in printed or written literary documents, using existing and available records as a means'; the ideal of efficiency 'exists when we are able to gather together a complete series of adequate bibliographical records on any given subject, and to collect, on the basis of these records, all existing records that we require for our investigation.'

13. Murray, David. 'Bibliography: Its Scope and Methods, with a View to the Work of a Local Bibliographical Society'. *Records of the Glasgow Bibliographical Society*, 1 (1914), 1–105. Inaugural essay for the group, the first part of which discusses the term, descriptive practices, and subject access in the light of an

extensive and thoughtful historical survey, the latter of which (pp. 51ff.) concern specifically the bibliography of Scotland and of Glasgow.

14. Feipel, Louis N. 'Elements of Bibliography'. *Papers of the Bibliographical Society of America*, 10 (1916), 175–93. Procedures and points of consideration for the compiler, well presented.

15. Rollins, Carl Purington. 'The Printing of Bibliographies'. *Papers of the Bibliographical Society of America*, 16 (1922), 107–17. The venerated designer for Yale University addresses matters of typographic design for bibliographical citations.

16. Schneider, Georg. 'Theoretisch-Geschichtlicher Teil', in his *Handbuch der Bibliographie* (Leipzig: Hiersemann, 1923; also in the '2. underänderte Auflage', 1924, in which some of the corrections on pp. 481–4 are incorporated into the text, as well as in the '3. Auflage', 1926), pp. 3–199. Essentially a philosophical and historical essay, with many valuable insights. Although this text is lacking in later eds of the *Handbuch* (beginning with the '4. gänzlich veränderte und stark vermehrte Auflage', 1930), the 1934 Shaw translation (21, below) is widely available.

17. Van Hoesen, Henry B., and Frank K. Walter. *Bibliography: Practical, Enumerative, Historical: An Introductory Manual.* New York, London: Scribner, 1928. A widely-used detailed overview of all aspects of bibliography, in which Chapter 2 (pp. 9–45) is devoted to 'Practical Bibliography', i.e., the compilation of lists.

18. Esdaile, Arundell. *A Student's Manual of Bibliography.* London: George Allen & Unwin; New York: Scribner, 1931. 2nd ed., 1932. 3rd ed., revised by Roy Stokes, 1954. 4th ed., now called *Esdaile's Manual of Bibliography*, revised by Roy Stokes, and issued in the U.S. by Barnes & Noble, New York, 1967. 5th revised ed., Metuchen, N.J.: Scarecrow Press, 1981. Originally

based on lectures by the British Museum reference specialist delivered to library students at University College, London, the book provides an overview of the history of book production and of the access to early books through bibliographies. The 1932 ed. adds a three-page list of addenda and corrigenda; the changes in the 1954 ed. are more extensive but still essentially cosmetic. With the 1967 and 1981 eds Stokes becomes the major figure, as the content reflects a greater need for generalization. Three chapters are relevant to this study. Those on collation and description summarize the history of the production of books and other written documents, along the way serving as a primer of descriptive bibliography of sorts. The chapter on the arrangement of bibliographies, expanded somewhat in the 1967 ed., is abandoned in the 1981 ed. in deference to Stokes's coverage of the topic in *The Function of Bibliography* (1969; 73. below).

19. Gaselee, Stephen. 'The Aims of Bibliography'. *The Library*, 4th series, 13 (1932), 225–50. In his presidential address for the Bibliographical Society, London, the Bibliographer of early church history and other topics briefly traces the history of enumerative bibliography, and identifies the bibliographer's activities: collection, enumeration, description, analysis, and conclusion. In his response, W. W. Greg objects (pp. 250–5): Gaselee's conception justifies the bibliographer's efforts merely as a service to other sciences and not as a science in its own right. A. W. Pollard (pp. 255–8) replies that both men 'want the same things: the question at issue is as to whether we want them *as bibliographers*, or in some other capacity'.

20. Fulton, John F. 'The Principles of Bibliographical Citation: An Informal Discourse Addressed to Writers of Scientific Papers'. *Medical Library Association Bulletin*, n.s., 22 (April 1934), 183–97. Terse, clear-headed, and enlightened discussion of the options.

21. Schneider, Georg. *Theory and History of Bibliography*. Translated by Ralph Robert Shaw. New York: Columbia Uni-

versity Press, 1934. A translation of 16, above, pedestrian perhaps but also serviceable, and unarguably a sound base for Shaw's brilliant visions over the subsequent decades.

22. Cowley, J. D. *Bibliographical Description and Cataloguing.* London: Grafton, 1939. A respected method for describing documents in general, superseded by later specialized efforts. By approaching its subject on broad and practical terms, and concerned as it is with matters of detail, the book can stress the commonalities and objectives of all kinds of descriptive work, and still come short of preaching the cause of their total integration.

23. Schrero, Morris. 'Bibliographic Technique'. *Special Libraries,* 30 (1939), 302–6. Working from the four requisites of accuracy, completeness, consistency, and arrangement, a Pittsburgh technology librarian describes the compiler's procedures in terms of the different kinds of material cited.

24. Higgins, Marion Villiers. *Bibliography: A Beginner's Guide to Making, Evaluation, and Use of Bibliographies.* New York: H. W. Wilson, 1941. A brief, convenient overview, still to be recommended for casual exposure and practical guidance.

25. Swank, Raynard. 'Subject Catalogs, Classifications, or Bibliographies: A Review of Critical Discussions, 1876–1942'. *Library Quarterly,* 14 (1944), 316–32. A historical survey of arguments over subject access through the three institutions in libraries.

26. Barnard, Cyril C. 'Bibliographical Citation'. *The Librarian and Book World,* 39 (1950), 105–10, 171–5, 191–5 (the latter four pp. mis-numbered as 125–9). Also issued separately and designated as '2nd ed.' (London: James Clarke, 1960). A thoughtful, practical overview of citation practices.

27. Shera, Jesse H., and Margaret E. Egan. *Bibliographic Organization: Papers presented before the Fifteenth Annual Conference of*

the Graduate Library School, July 24–29, 1950. Chicago: University of Chicago Press, 1951. (Unlike other such conferences, the proceedings of this one were not issued in *Library Quarterly*.) A landmark event; for whereas the cause of centralized bibliographical efforts had been promoted and praised for many years, only through the intellectual focus of this conference would the objectives catch the imagination of the library community (Dunkin below notwithstanding). The basic points are restated and reshaped in several other later writings by these authors, notably among them Shera's 'Bibliographic Management', *American Documentation*, 2 (1951), 47–54, and Egan and Shera's 'Foundations of a Theory of Bibliography', *Library Quarterly*, 22 (1952), 125–37. *See also* Shera's *Libraries and the Organization of Knowledge* (Hamden, Conn.: Archon Books, 1965), *passim.*, and for a reprint of the 1952 article, pp. 18–33. Reuben Peiss's review in *Library Quarterly*, 21 (1951), 229–30, is impressive.

28. Dunkin, Paul S. 'Foundations in the Sky', *Library Quarterly*, 23 (1953), 126–34. A response to Shera above, mixing red herrings with unsettling reservations, all the more provocatively thanks to a wicked sense of prose.

29. Kinney, Mary R. *Bibliographical Style Manuals: A Guide to Their Use in Documentation and Research.* (ACRL Monographs, 8.) Chicago: American Library Association, 1953. A useful evaluative list of the major statements.

30. Ranganathan, S. R. 'Universal Bibliography and its Substitutes', *Libri*, 2 (1953), 292–6. Of all the guru's clear-headed and cryptic pronouncements, this brief contrast of the different types of lists is perhaps most relevant to the present study.

31. Baer, Karl A. 'Bibliographical Methods in the Biological Sciences', *Special Libraries*, 45 (1954), 74–80. Seasoned observations by a pharmaceutical librarian, supporting 'microcosmic' efforts which may be still achievable through 'snowballing' techniques.

32. Collison, Robert L. 'The Bibliographer in the Library'. *Libri*, 4
     (1954), 308–14. The City of Westminster librarian, noted later
     for his reference book guides, calls for co-operative projects.

33. Freer, Percy. *Bibliography and Modern Book Production*. Johan-
     nesburg: Whitwatersrand University Press, 1954. Chapter 1
     (pp. 1–13), 'The Bibliographers Define Bibliography', is
     particularly useful as a survey of previous thought.

34. Reichardt, Gunther. 'Die Bedeutung der Annotation für
     Bibliographie und Katalog', in *Bibliothek, Bibliothekar, Bib-
     liothekswissenschaft: Festschrift Joris Vortius* (Leipzig: Harrass-
     owitz, 1954), pp. 86–109. A major essay in the German history
     of annotation practices.

35. Shaw, Ralph R. 'Mechanical and Electronic Aids for Bibliog-
     raphy'. *Library Trends*, 2 (1954), 522–31. An analytical study of
     the specific steps in the compiler's work, and the appropriate
     application of mechanization to each.

36. Wilson, William Jerome. 'Manuscript Cataloging'. *Traditio*, 6
     (1955), 457–555. While explicitly on a somewhat different
     topic, this superb essay is valuable to compilers, in particular as
     it suggests ways in which the detailing of the physical item can
     bring out characteristics of the content.

37. Bercaw, Louise O. 'Methodology used in Compiling a
     Bibliography in the Field of Agricultural Economics'. *A.L.A.
     Bulletin*, 30 (1956), 622–6. An American librarian stresses the
     need for a well conceived definition of scope in particular.

38. Eppelsheimer, Hanns W. 'Von der Würde bibliographischer
     Arbeit', in *Das Werck der Bücher: . . . Festschrift für Horst
     Kliemann* (Freiburg: Rombach, 1956), pp. 86–9. A brief
     appreciation in praise of bibliographical activities.

39. Harlow, Neal. 'The Well-Tempered Bibliographer'. *Papers of
     the Bibliographical Society of America*, 50 (1956), 28–39. Anec-

dotes and musings on work involving Americana in particular.

40. Clapp, Verner W. 'Bibliography', in *Encyclopedia Americana* (New York: Americana, 1957), vol. 3, pp. 674–7; on different pages in later eds, i.e., pp. 721–4 in the 1968–78 eds. A convenient overview with useful perspectives, particularly on the role of bibliographies in the bibliographical macrocosm, by one of the major participants at the 1950 Chicago conference.

41. Hodgson, James G. *Bibliographical Forms for Literary Citations.* Chicago: Department of the Army, Research and Engineering Command, Quartermaster Food and Container Institute for the Armed Forces, 1957. The imprint may be curious, but in fact the text shows an impressive competence and ultimately leaves one wondering about the primary purpose of the study in the first place.

42. Bourton, K. 'Subject Bibliographies and their Compilation'. *ASLIB Proceedings*, 11 (1959), 5–8. Practical advice from a compiler for a British manufacturer.

43. Bryon, J. F. W. 'Bibliographies in the Public Library'. *The Librarian and Book World*, 48 (1959), 29–33. A proposal for reporting selective holdings of bibliographies depending on the nature of the readership served.

44. Bryant, Margaret S. *Bibliographies, Abstracts, Indexes.* (Vol. 2, part 2, of 'The State of the Library Art', ed. by Ralph R. Shaw.) New Brunswick, N.J.: Rutgers–The State University, Graduate School of Library Science, 1960. General discussions of bibliography as defined in several ways, enlightened by early perspectives of information science, mostly on pp. 45–50.

45. Foskett, D. J. *Notes on Compiling Bibliographies for the Guidance of Students Preparing Reports and Theses in the Field of Education.* (Education Libraries Bulletin, Supplement no. 2.) London:

University of London, Institute of Education, 1960.* 2nd ed.,
1967. A summary handbook with practices directed at a
specialized readership.

46. Iyengar, T. K. S. 'Compiling a Bibliography', *Indian Librarian*,
    14 (1960), 165–9. The rudiments of the compiler's activities
    explained.

47. Piercy, Esther J. 'Is Bibliographic Standardization Possible?'
    Library Resources and Technical Services, 4 (1960), 67–70.
    Seasoned thoughts on the subject by a highly respected
    cataloguer.

48. Walford, A. J. 'The Plight of the Subject Bibliographer',
    Library Review, 17 (1960), 403–8. The compiler of the standard
    British guide to reference works reflects on the increasing
    complexity and specialization of the compiler's work.

49. Baer, Hans. *Bibliographie und bibliographische Arbeitstechnik:
    Eine Einführung*. Frauenfeld: Huber, 1961. A well conceived
    textbook mostly on the use of existing lists, with some
    discussion of the work of compilation, mostly related to
    library cataloguing practices.

50. Arlt, Gustave O. 'Bibliography — An Essential Piece of Equip-
    ment', *Library Journal*, 86 (1961), 1539–41. An American
    professor calls for better recognition of the importance of lists
    in scholarly communication.

51. Thompson, Lawrence S. *Who Killed Bibliography?* (Occasional
    Contributions, vol. 13, no. 3.) Lexington: University of
    Kentucky Library, 1962.* Re-issued, Berkeley, Cal.: Peacock
    Press, 1965. A brief polemical essay by an eminent American
    academic librarian, addressing the mortal symptoms of 'in-
    accuracy, indifference to detail, inconsistency, butchery of
    foreign languages, imperfect concepts of publishing traditions,
    and use of heresay and secondary evidence'. The assassins and
    would-be assassins are identified as (1) bibliographical senti-

mentalists, whose infatuated but passive reading leads to a low regard for accuracy; (2) the linguistic illiterates, who 'generally treat their mother tongue the more cruelly for not knowing other languages'; (3) the folklore of gadgetry, which fails to comprehend that mechanization only facilitates tasks that remain 'essential handmaidens to bibliographical research', without addressing the 'higher bibliographical tasks ... that will give us an inner sense of conviction'; and (4) 'an alleged tradition of democracy in the world of education', which neglects and stifles the appropriate and necessary concern for the historical contexts and intellectual traditions at stake. 'Recognition and respect for the fundamental ingredients of scholarship' will offer a turning point for improved conditions.

52. Weitzel, Rolf. *Bibliographische Suchspraxis: Eine Einführung*. Stuttgart: Poeschel, 1962. A Swiss university librarian describes the rudiments of searching techniques, especially for early books, along the way reflecting on the special features of bibliographies in general.

53. Köth, Arno. *Wie ermittele ich, schnell, sicher, genau, Buch- und Zeitschriftentitel: Eine methodische Einführung in die praktische Arbeit mit Bibliographien*. Köln: Selbstverlag, 1963. How to make and use them—as the title suggests—speedy, safe and specific.

54. Robinson, A. M. Lewin. *Systematic Bibliography: A Practical Guide to the Work of Compilation*. Cape Town: University of Cape Town, School of Librarianship, 1963.* Revised ed., Cape Town: Juta, 1966;* London: Clive Bingley, 1966. 3rd revised ed., London: Clive Bingley; Hamden, Conn.: Linnet Books, 1971. 4th ed., London: Clive Bingley; Munich, New York, Paris: K. G. Saur, 1979. A major textbook on the compilation of bibliographies, somewhat more practical in its orientation than the present text. Some of the changes in the text over the course of the editions are detailed in references in the present book.

55. Wynar, Bohdan. *Introduction to Bibliography and Reference Books.* 'Preliminary ed.', Denver: University of Denver, Graduate School of Librarianship, 1963. 2nd ed., 1964. 3rd ed., revised and enlarged, newly titled *Introduction to Bibliography and Reference Work*, Denver: Libraries Unlimited, 1966. 4th revised ed., Rochester, N.Y.: Libraries Unlimited, 1967. A general textbook for library students, with a discussion of lists and their preparation on pp. 17–29 of the 1963 ed., extensively expanded on pp. 33–52 (esp. pp. 42–7) of the 1966 ed., and somewhat further extended on pp. 44–66 of the 1967 ed.

56. Shaw, Ralph R. 'Integrated Bibliography: Another View'. *Pennsylvania Library Association Bulletin*, 19 (1964), 20–4. Also published as 'Integrated Bibliography', *Library Journal*, 90 (1965), 819–22. Further thoughts on the systematization of the steps in the description of library materials.

57. Boehm, Eric H. *Blueprint for Bibliography: A System for the Social Sciences and Humanities.* Santa Barbara: Clio Press, 1965. Six recommendations for creating 'one integrated, comprehensive international bibliographical system for the social sciences and humanities.'

58. Goltz, Marianne. 'Probleme der Annotierung künstlericher Literatur in Katalogen und empfehlenden Bibliographien'. *Bibliotheksarbeit heute*, 3 (1965), 91–108. Recommendations and value judgments in the annotations for literature on artistic topics.

59. Hibberd, Lloyd. 'Physical and Reference Bibliography'. *The Library*, 5th series, 20 (1965), 124–34. An American musicologist and book collector proposes an overview of the various activities subsumed under the name of bibliography.

60. Waligora, Lorenz. 'Die Annotation als Erschliessungsmittel'. *Der Bibliothekar*, 19 (1965), 23–30; 20 (1966), 3–12. Continuation of the discussion among German librarians of the role of annotations in bibliographical description.

61. Rost, Gottfried. *Bibliographie und Bibliograph: Eine Literaturinformation über Formen und Methoden der Bibliographie, mit einem Ausblick auf die elektronische Verarbeitung bibliographischer Daten.* (Bibliographischer Informationsdienst der Deutschen Bücherei, 10.) Leipzig: Deutsche Bücherei, 1966. A general survey of the goals and procedures involved in bibliographical citations.

62. Saur, Karl Gerhard, and Josef Ferring. *Bibliographieren leicht gemacht, Teil I: Grundbegriffe: Teil II: Praktische Anwendung.* Düsseldorf: Verlag der Jugendbuchhandel, 1966. A brief exposition of basic principles and practices.

63. Dux, Werner. *Method und Technik der Bearbeitung und Nützung von Bibliographien.* (Einführung in die Information und Dokumentation, 11.) Leipzig: VEB Bibliographisches Institut, 1967. An introductory manual for compilers and users of lists.

64. Kinney, Mary R. *The Abbreviated Citation: A Bibliographical Problem.* (ACRL Monographs, 28.) Chicago: American Library Association, 1967. By approaching the problem of cryptic statements in terms of the specialities themselves, this text in effect becomes a guide of sorts to the literature, at least as it can be clarified through 109 reference sources.

65. Shoemaker, Richard H. 'Bibliography (General)'. *Library Trends*, 15 (1967), 340–6. A survey of the state of the art in 1967, one of a series of essays on coverage in several dozen major subject areas.

66. Staveley, Ronald, Ia C. McIlwaine and John H. St.J. McIlwaine. *Introduction to Subject Study.* London: André Deutsch, 1967. A librarian's survey of particular disciplines, with discussions of the distinctive literatures, perspectives and reference sources involved.

67. Stokes, Roy. *Bibliographical Control and Service.* London: André Deutsch, 1967. A leader in the world of bibliography

discusses the objectives and characteristics of our bibliographical record.

68. Domay, Friedrich. *Formenlehre der bibliographischen Ermittlung: Eine Einführung in die Praxis der Litteraturerschliessung.* Stuttgart: Anton Hiersemann, 1968. A method book for citing and using bibliographical references.

69. Tanselle, G. Thomas. 'A Proposal for Recording Additions to Bibliographies'. *Papers of the Bibliographical Society of America*, 62 (1968), 227–36. Suggestion of a clearing-house for purposes of updating and correcting standard bibliographies.

70. Wilson, Patrick. *Two Kinds of Power: An Essay in Bibliographical Control.* (Contributions to Librarianship, 5.) Berkeley, Los Angeles: University of California Press, 1968. A philosophical discussion exploring the assumptions and consequences of our bibliographical programmes and attitudes. The prose itself is such as to suggest an attempt to uncover the eighth kind of ambiguity; but the sense of this landmark essay is well worth the effort. Its influence has been considerable: *see*, for instance, Bates (91. below).

71. Blum, Rudolf. 'Bibliographie, eine Wort- und Begriffsgeschichtliche Untersuchung'. *Archiv für Geschichte des Buchwesens*, 10 (1969–70), 1016–1246. Translated by Mathilde V. Rovelstad as *Bibliographia: An Inquiry into its Definition and Designations* (Chicago: American Library Association, 1980). An historical survey of the term and concept. For all its impressive erudition, the study remains quite unnecessarily parochial in its perspectives, as suggested in the review by John Feather in the *Times Literary Supplement* for December 26, 1980, p. 1472.

72. Stokes, Roy. 'Bibliography', in *Encyclopedia of Library and Information Science*, vol. 2 (New York: Marcel Dekker, 1969), pp. 407–19. A convenient epitome of the viewpoints developed more fully in Stokes's revisions of Esdaile and other books (18. and 67. above, 73. below).

73. Stokes, Roy. *The Function of Bibliography.* London: André Deutsch, 1969. 2nd ed., Aldershot, Hants.: Gower, 1982. A detailed discussion of the basic objectives of and essential interrelationships between the various specialities of bibliography.

74. Hackman, Martha. *The Practical Bibliographer.* Englewood Cliffs, N.J.: Prentice-Hall, 1970. A general guide for the use of books and libraries, particularly useful for training of searchers. Chapter 8 (pp. 89–115) is devoted to 'Bibliographic Citation'.

75. Hale, Barbara M. *The Subject Bibliography of the Social Sciences and Humanities.* Oxford: Pergamon Press, 1970. A survey of the growth of the bibliographical record, concentrating on major works and hence, essentially superficial, but still thoughtfully done and very much worth consulting.

76. Needham, Christopher D. *The Study of Subject Bibliography, with Special Reference to the Social Sciences.* (Student Contribution Series, no. 3.) College Park: University of Maryland, School of Library and Information Services, 1970. A library student seminar served as the basis for this attempt to identify basic principles.

77. Vianello, Nereo. *La citazione di opere a stampa e manoscritti.* (Biblioteconomia e bibliografia, Saggi e studi, 6.) Firenze: Olschki, 1970. Analysis and explanation of citation practices.

78. Schiødt, Nanna. 'Bibliografi', in *Sigurdiana: Sigurd Berg 75 år* (København, 1971), pp. 20–31. Personal memoirs and viewpoints of a compiler, as part of a semi-private Festschrift for a specialist in historic music instruments.

79. Boehm, Eric H. 'On the Second Knowledge: A Manifesto for the Humanities'. *Libri*, 22 (1972), 312–23. A further argument in support of Boehm's *Blueprint* (57. above), stressing the need for improved bibliographic access.

80. Richmond, Phyllis A. 'Document Description and Representation'. *Annual Review of Information Science and Technology*, 7 (1972), 73–102. A laudable search for principles underlying citation practices of all kind, along with a critical evaluation of codes and policies.

81. Crossman, E. J. and Cheryl D. Goodchild. 'A Way to Ease Preparation of Checklists and Bibliographies'. *Scholarly Publishing*, 4 (1973), 245–9. Description of conveniences in the paperwork activities of the compiler, involving a system of tabbed strips.

82. Simon, H. R. 'Analysis of Bibliographies'. *Library Trends*, issue for July 1973 (vol. 22, no. 1; pp. 1–74). Essays on the character of and relationships between bibliographies, as discernable through research studies.

83. Anderson, Dorothy. *Universal Bibliographic Control: A Long Term Policy, A Plan for Action.* München/Pullach: Verlag Dokumentation, 1974. From this proposal has developed the plan for implementation of Universal Bibliographic Control, through national bibliographies and library cataloguing activities as co-ordinated through the International Federation of Library Associations.

84. Besterman, Theodore. *Fifty Years a Bookman.* (Arundell Esdaile Lecture for 1973.) London: The Library Association, 1974. The venerable compiler here expresses a variety of opinions, some of them conspicuously sound, and describes some of his adventures.

85. Mangouni, Norman. 'An International Style for Bibliographic References'. *Scholarly Publishing*, 5 (1974), 239–54. A call for standardization, based on cataloguing models.

86. Picard, Berthold. 'Bibliographie und Bibliographien'. Chapter 6 in the *Handbuch des Buchhandels, Band I: Allgemeines*, ed. by Horst Machill (Hamburg: Verlag für Buchmarkt-

Forschung, 1974), pp. 250–314. A thorough and far-ranging survey, mostly for the book trade but in fact useful to compilers in general, with many topics relevant to citation practice presented in detail.

87. Spencer, H., Linda Reynolds and B. Coe, 'Typographic Coding in Lists and Bibliographies'. *Applied Ergonomics*, 5 (1974), 136–41. Studies in the layout, typography and design of bibliographies, conducted through the Royal College of Art, for purposes of enhancing the ease of access to statements. *See also* their 'Spatial and Typographic Coding in Printed Bibliographical Materials', *Journal of Documentation*, 32 (1975), 59–70.

88. Tanselle, G. Thomas. 'Bibliography and Science'. *Studies in Bibliography*, 27 (1974), 55–89. An exploration of the ways in which the various activities performed by bibliographers may be viewed as scientific in their procedures and functions.

89. Brenni, Vito J. *Essays on Bibliography*. Metuchen, N.J.: Scarecrow Press, 1975. Reprints of major essays in systematic and analytical bibliography, including several of the titles cited earlier.

90. Davinson, Donald. *Bibliographic Control*. London: Clive Bingley; Hamden, Conn.: Linnet Books, 1975. 2nd ed., London: Clive Bingley, 1981. A survey of bibliographic resources, such as cumulatively provide bibliographic control, usefully conceived here according to type of list or of material covered. A concluding chapter provides rudimentary guidance in matters of 'Bibliographic Compilation and Bibliographic Citation', i.e., Chapter 13 (pp. 111–16) in the 1975 ed., Chapter 18 (pp. 145–57) in the 1981 ed.

91. Bates, Marcia J. 'Rigorous Systematic Bibliography'. *RQ*, 16 (1976), 7–26. The rigor in question is to be achieved through an application of five specifications set forth by Wilson (70. above), as discussed specifically in the present volume.

92. Francis, F. C. 'Bibliography', in *Encyclopaedia Britannica*, 15th ed. (Chicago: Encyclopaedia Britannica, 1976), 'Macropaedia', vol. 2, pp. 978–81. A useful brief survey, with suggestions for compilers included.

93. Kumar, Girje, and Krishan Kumar. *Bibliography*. New Delhi: Vikas Publishing House, 1976. Chapter 16 (pp. 200–14) is devoted to the 'Mechanics of Compiling and Arranging a Bibliography'.

94. *Prospects for Change in Bibliographic Control: Proceedings of the Thirty-Eighth Annual Conference of the Graduate Library School, November 8–9, 1976*. Chicago: University of Chicago Press, 1977; also issued as vol. 47, no. 1 (1977) of *Library Quarterly*. Sequel in a sense to the watershed conference of 1950 (27 above), less monumental in its impact perhaps, but with due if tangential cognizance of enumerative bibliographies. Doralyn Hickey's paper, 'Theory of Bibliographic Control in Libraries' (pp. 19–39) is particularly notable.

95. Olschki, Alessandro. 'Sua maestà la citazione: un invito agli autori, ai docenti, agli editori'. *La bibliofilia*, 79 (1977), 277–82. A call for writers to be more responsible in their citation practices, with comments added by the editor Roberto Ridolfi.

96. Tanselle, G. Thomas. 'Descriptive Bibliography and Library Cataloguing'. *Studies in Bibliography*, 30 (1977), 1–56. A critical evaluation of the first ed. of the Anglo-American Cataloguing Rules, in terms of the rules in addressing the needs of bibliographers who study the physical book.

97. Williamson, Nancy Joyce. *Cataloguing and Bibliography: A Comparative Study of their Interrelationships as Seen through their Principles and Practices*. Ph.D. dissertation, Case-Western Reserve University, 1977. UMi film 77–25,205. A study of the conventional differences in citation styles between the two, based on a limited but well selected choice of bibliographies, and effectively argued in its conclusions.

98. Batts, Michael S. *The Bibliography of German Literature: An Historical and Critical Survey.* (Kanadische Studien zur deutschen Sprache und Literatur, 19.) Bern: Peter Lang, 1978. A history of German bibliographical practices from the Renaissance to the present, from Gesner to the computer.

99. Bryer, Jackson R. 'From Second-Class Citizenship to Respectability: The Odyssey of an Enumerative Bibliographer'. *Literary Research Newsletter*, 3 (1978), 55–61. A compiler of literary bibliographies describes his achievements and defends his good efforts.

100. Frank, Peter R. *Von der systematischen Bibliographie zur Dokumentation.* (Wege zur Forschung, 144.) Darmstadt: Wissenschaftliche Buchgesellschaft, 1978. An anthology, including reprints of several titles cited above, arranged so as to suggest an inexorable historical sequence, but with useful commentary. The bibliography on pp. 495–520 is particularly valuable.

101. Thompson, Margaret. 'Incorrect Citations: A Problem and a Challenge for Librarians'. *Australian Academic and Research Libraries*, vol. 9, no. 3 (1978), 45–7. Strategies used in reference work to circumvent an annoying nuisance.

102. Hickey, Doralyn. 'The American Librarian's Dream: Full Bibliographic Control with Complete Freedom of Access'. *University of Tennessee Library Lectures*, 28–30 (1976–78), 14–31. In the 1977 lecture, a respected theorist describes the objectives of the ideal catalogue and bibliographical record.

103. Krummel, D. W., and John Bruce Howell. 'Bibliographical Standards and Style'. *Scholarly Publishing*, 10 (1979), 223–40. The impetus for the present book, which grows out of an evaluation of the strength and limitations of the American National Standard for Bibliographical References.

104. Colaianne, A. J. 'The Aims and Methods of Annotated

Bibliography'. *Scholarly Publishing*, 11 (1980), 321–33. While the main concern is annotation, the concept is interpreted broadly, so as to address an ample range of topics basic to the compiler's intention in preparing a bibliography in the first place.

105. DeAmorim, Maria J. *Bibliographic References: A Critique of Style Manuals for the Preparation of Theses and Dissertations.* Ph.D. dissertation, Case-Western Reserve University, 1980. UMi film 81–00,528. An evaluation of the citation style prescribed in forty-eight manuals, with recommendation for improvements through a better cognizance of library cataloguing practices.

106. Hyatt, Dennis. 'Writer's Guides to Periodicals in the Social Sciences: Quasi-Bibliography and the Decline of Subject Bibliography'. *Behavioral and Social Sciences Librarian*, 1 (1980), 201–5. A review essay of five bibliographical guidebooks, which proposes that their genre 'may be the most likely survivors from a more leisurely past'.

107. London, Gertrude. 'The Place and Role of Bibliographic Description in General and Individual Catalogues: A Historical Analysis'. *Libri*, 30 (1980), 253–84. An extended summary of the descriptive practices proposed in library cataloguing codes, from the mid-nineteenth century to today.

108. Harmon, Robert R. *Elements of Bibliography: A Simplified Approach.* Metuchen, N.J.: Scarecrow Press, 1981. The work of the compiler is addressed in chapters 5–7 (pp. 58–98), devoted to 'The Nature and Uses of Enumerative Bibliography', 'Forms and Functions of Enumerative Bibliography' and 'Compiling an Enumerative Bibliography'.

109. Sable, Martin H. 'Systematic Bibliography as the Reflection of Reality'. *International Library Review*, 13 (1981), 17–24. An out-of-date bibliography, in effect, is a testimony to earlier states of knowledge: an interesting perspective.

110. Evans, Martha M. 'Bibliographic Control of Large Quantities of Research Material'. *RQ*, 23 (1983), 393–9. Pragmatic advice based on experience in compiling an extended bibliography on dyslexia.

Index